youth

REINVENTING
CO-OPERATIVES

young perspectives on the international co-operative movement

edited by: julia smith, robin puga, ian macpherson.

Cover and layout design by Melinda Skeels.

10 9 8 7 6 5 4 3 2 1

Printed in Winnipeg, Canada

Library and Archives Canada Cataloguing in Publication Data

Youth reinventing co-operatives : young perspectives on the international co-operative movement / edited by Julia Smith, Robin Puga, Ian MacPherson.

ISBN 1-55058-307-7

1. Cooperative societies--Case studies. 2. Youth in development--Case studies. 3. Student cooperatives--Case studies. I. Smith, Julia, 1981- II. Puga, Robin, 1975- III. MacPherson, Ian, 1939- IV. British Columbia Institute for Co-operative Studies

HD2963.Y68 2005   334'.083   C2005-903982-5

British Columbia Institute for Co-operative Studies
University of Victoria
University House 2 - room 109
PO Box 3060 STN CSC
Victoria, BC V8W 3R4
tel. (250)472-4539
email: rochdale@uvic.ca
website: http://web.uvic.ca/bcics

DEDICATION

To the youthful minds that made
the preparation of this book
possible, necessary and pleasurable.

PREFACE

The ICA values young people and the many different contributions they can make to the Co-op movement. In fact a lot of people now involved in the ICA were involved in youth co-operation first, showing that young people really do become the leaders of tomorrow.

We mustn't forget how relevant young people are in today's world. Young people face a lot of the world's problems and what is very positive is how they are using co-operation to overcome these. The creativity and increased focus on social issues brings a fresh edge to the International Co-operative movement and is something we can all learn from and be inspired by.

This book highlights the diversity of co-operative activities that young people are engaged in and shows that young people are not restricted just to being involved in youth co-operatives. Young people are working in a wide range of different areas and they naturally often branch out into wholly new areas of co-operative life.

More and more young people are making the choice to live and work co-operatively, but we need more education on what the international co-operative movement can offer. This book is a great way of showing people what is already being achieved by young people and what they are dreaming for the future.

The ICA Youth Network

ACKNOWLEDGEMENTS

We at the British Columbia Institute for Co-operative Studies have been very pleased to be associated with the development of this book.

We would like to thank the International Labour Organisation, particularly Jürgen Schwettmann, Head of the Co-op Branch, for the financial support that made its preparation possible. We would also like to thank our other partners, the International Co-operative Alliance and the Canadian Co-operative Association for their help and encouragement. We particularly appreciate the support of Garry Cronan and Jan- Erik Embsen at the ICA and Joanne Ferguson at the CCA. We are indebted to the support of the African Region of the International Co-operative Alliance for allowing Julia Smith to have time to work on the project while she has been serving as a Canadian Co-operative Association intern in the Nairobi office.

We are also particularly indebted to Dr. Andrea Levin from University of Buenos Aires in Argentina, who generously helped in securing case studies from her country, to Sarah Groot who assisted in securing the cases from Ghana and to Ursula Titus from the Umsobomvu Youth Fund for helping to prepare the cases from South Africa.

On behalf of BCICS, I would like to thank Julia Smith for her work in encouraging many of the submissions and helping edit the work; Robin Puga, from the British Columbia Institute for Co-operative Studies for his work with the photographs, editing and preparation of the manuscript; and Melinda Skeels for her work in laying it out for publication. We would also like to acknowledge with thanks the support of the Maureen Robinson Memorial Fund in assisting us in printing this book.

Most of all, we would like to thank all the young people who took the time to prepare their stories and reflect on the co-operative movement and how it is affecting, or could affect, their lives.

Ian MacPherson
Director

CONTENTS

Part Two: Youth Developing Co-operatives

Part Three:
Co-operatives Encouraging Youth Involvement

Part Four: Conclusions And Recommendations

FOREWORD

In September 2000, the largest gathering of Heads of State and Government the world has ever seen met at the Millennium Summit to adopt the Millennium Declaration. They resolved to "develop and implement strategies that give young people everywhere a real chance to find decent and productive work." This resolution gave birth to the Youth Employment Network (YEN) formed by the United Nations, the World Bank and the ILO, which acts as the Network's secretariat.

Two years later, the UN General Assembly adopted a resolution entitled "Promoting youth employment", and in November 2003, the ILO Governing Body identified youth employment as a topic for a general discussion at the International Labour Conference in June 2005. In preparation for this general discussion, the ILO organized a Tripartite Meeting on Youth Employment: *The Way Forward* in October 2004.

These are clear indicators that youth employment has become a top priority for the ILO and its tripartite constituents.

The ILO has been bound up with the international co-operative movement since the organisation's earliest days. Its first Director-General, Mr Albert Thomas, served on the board of the International Cooperative Alliance and established a Cooperative Branch as early as 1920. Its constitution confers a permanent observer status to the global co-operative movement as represented by the ICA.

In June 2002, the International Labour Conference adopted *Recommendation 193 on the Promotion of Cooperatives*, thus reasserting the importance of co-operatives for the world of work. In February 2004, the ICA and the ILO signed a Memorandum of Understanding and a Common Cooperative Agenda to boost their joint efforts in fighting poverty and creating decent work worldwide.

We are therefore very happy to team up with the British Columbia Institute for Co-operative Studies, the ICA and the Canadian Co-operative Association in publishing a book that addresses both issues simultaneously: youth employment and co-operative development. The many case studies from around the world included in this book show that co-operatives are indeed a viable option for young people to find – or to create – gainful employment through collective action.

Perhaps even more important is the fact that the co-operative way of working seems to be more in line with the dreams, aspirations and convictions of young people than other forms of business. The democratic nature of the co-operative enterprise encourages participation, broadens ownership and fosters empowerment of youth, thus strengthening civil society while contributing to a growing economy.

This book presents ample evidence that co-operatives create the kind of jobs that the ILO would qualify as "Decent Work": that is, opportunities for women and men to obtain decent and productive work, in conditions of freedom, equity, security and human dignity. It is therefore an important contribution to the design of future youth employment promotion programmes.

Jürgen Schwettmann
Chief, Cooperatives Branch
International Labour Orgnisation

INTRODUCTION

There are at least four ways in which one might think about the theme of "co-operatives and young people".

First, one can consider examples of how young people are organizing co-operatives to meet their own needs: to find employment, to learn how to succeed in the market place, and to help them as they obtain an education. The following pages, which are at best a partial snapshot of all the activities undertaken by young people in the international co-operative movement, provide several examples of this kind of activity.

Second, one can find examples of how some existing co-operatives are reaching out in various ways to involve young people, as participating members, as elected officials and as members of special groups. They undertake these initiatives for a number of reasons:
- they wish to "secure youth business;"
- they want to ensure the succession of young people in both elected and management positions;
- they are carrying on a co-operative tradition of youth involvement; and
- they recognize that youth issues are among the most important of those facing the communities they serve.

Third, one can seek to understand the dynamics of the relationship between youth and the co-operative movement by considering how the great economic and social issues of our time are affecting the development of co-operatives, both established and new. Young people are inevitably carriers of contemporary issues. As much as any group in global society, they feel the pressures of hunger, pandemics, social dislocation and war. They live with the certainty that they will suffer more than any other group from the growing ravages of environmental degradation.

Even more urgently, young people today bear an unacceptable proportion of the burden of unemployment. According to a recent study by the International Labour Organisation, young people aged fifteen to twenty-four, though only twenty-five per cent of the world's population, account for nearly fifty per cent of its unemployed: "in other words" 47 per cent of the total 186 millions unemployed in 2003.[1] And, of those 550 million of the world's working poor who are employed at rates that cannot provide an acceptable standard of living – the so-called "working poor" – young people account for 24 per cent or 130 millions.

The interest in co-operatives, therefore, among young people is driven by acute needs. This creates an immense challenge and an even greater opportunity for the international co-operative movement, particularly in the less industrialized parts of the world, the places where many of the case studies in this book are located and the places where the great majority of young people can be found.

Fourth, some young people bring to the co-operative world a deep determination to use co-operative solutions as one key to solving the issues of their times; the same kind of determination their ancestors demonstrated in building co-operatives, from Rochdale to Gujarat, from Flammersfeld to Regina and from Lima to Kobe. Their messages are not always comforting and they can be harshly critical, but that does not mean they are wrong or should be ignored.

Many youth, however, are inherently optimistic, and one can readily finds the kind of buoyant optimism, determination and idealism that youth have always contributed to the co-operative movement and to society generally. It is obvious in the reflections that several writers provide in the pages that immediately follow; it percolates through the case studies that are included thereafter. It is clear in their determination to find ways to develop organisations that reflect the values they believe are most important in the modern world. It is clear in the honest, sometimes biting, criticism they level at those who are handing on the co-operative trust.

The voices that follow come almost entirely from people who are under the age of thirty; in a few cases, they are from people recalling the time when they were – the time when they first became involved with co-operatives, the beginnings of lifetimes of commitment. One suspects that thirty years hence, many of the other authors in this book, wizened by decades of involvement in the co-operative movement, will be able to write similar reflections.

The Editors

---

1   International Labour Office, *Global Employment Trends for Youth* (Geneva: International Labour Organisation, 2004), p.1.

PART ONE:

Considering Co-operatives

It is both easy and difficult to think about co-operatives. They are almost everywhere around the world, in every country and meeting hundreds of different kinds of needs. One can find them in virtually every kind of community. Yet the information about them is often repetitive and tends to be concerned with co-operatives that have been successful in the past and still exist in the market place. Information about new co-operatives is rarely easy to locate. Many co-operatives, moreover, are not careful about communicating what is "different" about them and are focused almost entirely on the transactions they hope to have with members and customers. It is not surprising, then, that many young people – and older ones too – conduct business with co-operatives but do not readily know that they do so.[1] Nor can young people generally find out about them in the course of their academic studies: in most countries it is difficult, in some impossible, to find out about them in school curricula. In short, it takes some efforts by people, old and young, to understand the past accomplishments, common problems and future potential of co-operatives, a rather puzzling circumstance for a movement so widely spread and so frequently used.

The following papers reflect some of the ideas and attitudes of young people who, despite the intentional and unconscious barriers, have been considering the co-operative model from a number of different perspectives. They differ remarkably in tone and method. Some are intensely personal, reflecting deep commitments and extensive involvement. One of them, by Professor Mirta Vuoto, starts a long overdue analysis of youth attitudes towards co-operatives, using careful analytical techniques: it provides considerable food for thought, both for those who would teach about co-operatives and for those who would seek to engage more youth in the co-operative movement. Another, by Nicole Ghanie can be seen in the long tradition of social engagement that has characterized much of co-operative history. She raises a high bar for anyone

---

1   In over five years of instruction in a course on co-operative history at the University of Victoria only 20 per cent of the students registered in the course each year knew that they belonged to a co-operative. In reality, though, once local and regional co-operatives were identified, over 60 per cent realized that they had memberships in one co-operative or another. Similarly, many of the 15,000,000 members of Canadian co-operatives are not aware of the differences between co-operatives and other kinds of institutions. In many countries, older generations of people involved in co-operatives have not done a good job in communicating knowledge of their movement to succeeding generations. Basically, the "young" in recent times have had to find out for themselves, a sad reflection on the work of the co-operators who preceded them and of the educational institutions that have, with few exceptions around the world, consistently ignored the co-operative movement, its roles and contributions.

engaged in co-operatives, asking what it can and should do in the face of a major contemporary catastrophe. It is not, however, a barrier – just more obviously pressing – than those great issues of poverty and alienation that co-operators of another time have been willing to take on. Erik Haensel presents a road map for anyone wishing to pursue the most common form of communication away from home today.

Some authors speak from deep within the movement; others are "newcomers", meaning that the papers collectively present, in the historic traditions of co-operative discourse, a number of debates between what is and what should be, between limited and broad purposes, between the present, the past and the future.

The Editors

Jo Bibby Scullion, United Kingdom

Jo Bibby-Scullion is a student of politics at Edinburgh University. She has been involved in various aspects of the co-operative movement since the age of six. In 2003 she became the first young person to sit on the ICA Board; she has a special interest in organising global youth co-operation.

1 THINKING Globally

Jo Bibby Scullion

Young people are increasingly important. According to the United Nations (UN), children and young people, under the age of twenty-five, make up fifty percent of the world's population. The world has already begun to change to incorporate these billions of young people, by making more of an effort to engage them. Young people are going to have to start playing a larger part economically, socially and politically than they have been accustomed to in the recent past. Unfortunately, young people are also facing their share of problems: for example, one in four people under 25 years old lives in poverty.

So what can co-operatives offer young people?

The United Nation's Millennium Development Goals specify the need for decent and productive work for young people, especially in developing countries. This is a key area where co-operatives can help. In some areas of the world, co-operatives provide the only opportunities for young people to gain decent employment. The co-operative model can benefit young people who want to start up their own businesses but have little capital. Co-ops can provide support, advice and, in some countries, start up grants to help new co-operatives give young people the opportunity to be independent and to take the responsibility for their lives into their own hands. The International Co-operative Alliance (ICA) and the International Labour Organisation (ILO) recognise this and are working together to try and develop a program of decent work for young people who choose to use the co-operative model to meet their economic and social needs.

> Young people are drawn to the values and principles of the co-operative movement

Young people are drawn to the values and principles of the co-operative movement and are looking for a fair way of doing business. They value the fact that co-operatives contribute to the community and, in some countries, they have been able to turn to co-operatives as they search for ways to pursue ethical careers, particularly when they are looking for their first jobs.

Co-operatives provide work for young people, both within existing, established co-operatives and through those that young people organize and operate themselves. Co-operative values mean – or should mean – that young people are seen as equals and are encouraged to take an active and responsible part within the movement. Co-operatives can be helpful in assisting young people prepare for their working lives, either within co-ops or outside of them, through training and education programmes that empower young people. Most co-operatives are committed to providing employee and member training and education.

In some parts of the world co-operative schools are very common and provide many opportunities for young people: for example, in Malaysia school co-operatives play an important part in the national curriculum. They run student unions, câfés and shops, and they teach young people democratic leadership skills as they learn how to run a co-operative.

The same is true of co-operative housing. It is often one of the only choices for young people starting off in life on their own, while other people may choose it because of the social assets of living co-operatively. The North American Students Co-operative Organisation (NASCO) helps young people run successful and affordable student housing; a set of tasks that also offers the students chances to play leadership roles in their community.

> Co-operatives can help young people improve their lives.

So co-operatives can help young people improve their lives. Over the past few years, while people have started to accept that co-ops can be beneficial for youth, people have often asked me, in a slightly sceptical tone 'so what *can* young people do for co-operatives?' This is superficially quite a difficult question to answer without falling back on banalities. The fact that the question is being asked at all suggests that co-ops have not yet adequately accepted younger people. Change the question to 'so what *can* older people do for co-ops?' or indeed 'so what *can* white men do for co-ops?' and the problem (and indeed potential offensiveness) of the phrasing of the question becomes clearer. The question should be, "how are co-ops missing out, if a whole sector of the population is not encouraged and able to play their full role in the movement?"

One of the key answers that people focus on, however, is the challenge of planning for the effective succession of leaders; without that, the movement will surely decline. Equally important is the fact that, by failing to incorporate fifty percent of the population, the movement is missing out on many different and new perspectives and ideas. In the words of the 2003 ICA Europe youth conference,

"We (young people) are not the future, we are the present. Young people bring energy and vitality to the movement and often have an increased focus on the original values and principles. These are the things that make the co-operative movement stand out and are also one of the main aspects that attracts young people. The Co-op's aim of balancing economics and social concerns is unique."

> Young people bring energy and vitality to the movement and often have an increased focus on the original values and principles.

Within the co-op movement there has been such a change since its beginning in Rochdale, United Kingdom. When the British movement went through its permanent creation, most of the recorded Rochdale pioneers were neither young nor female. Now the movement spans 91 countries and involves young and old, men and women, in co-operation. Diversity gives us strength and that is why the co-operative movement is looking to encourage more young people to get involved. In 2003, the International Co-operative Alliance took an historic step by encouraging a young person to sit on the ICA's main decision-making board. I had the privilege of being the first young person, and I have seen, all around the world, the difference young people can make. Young people do not want to take over the movement; we just want the chance to shape part of our movement, and to try and continue the co-operative values and principles. We have a lot to offer and can help the co-operative movement grow in new and exciting ways. Co-operation is the key, whether it is between old and young, male and female, rich and poor.

Lee Wilson,
Australia

Lee Wilson works with the Australian Centre for
Cooperative Research and Development (ACCORD)
as a Research Assistant. ACCORD is a joint venture
between the University of Technology, Sydney,
Charles Sturt University and the NSW Department
of Fair Trading. Lee is involved in research analysis
for papers on the formation of New Cooperatives
and the potential for cooperative models to fill 'un-
met need' gaps in housing and aged care facilities.

How could co-operatives become more important in the future?

Lee Wilson

The dual purpose of this essay is to raise questions about the role of young people in the co-operative movement and to introduce issues surrounding the socio-political environment in Australia that could affect decisions young people might make in thinking about becoming involved in co-operatives. Unfortunately, the attitudes and behaviours of young people towards co-operatives have not been closely studied, nor is it easy to ascertain how many young people are "active" members of current co-operatives. It is possible, however, to see the potential for young people to actualize their feelings towards relevant social movements in practical terms by either joining existing co-operatives or by setting up their own.

Melucci describes identifying with social movements as being an emotional investment, which "enables individuals to feel like part of a common unity."[1] Furthermore, "participation in forms of collective mobilization or in social movements, involvements

---

1   A. Melucci, "The process of collective identity," from *Social movements and culture*, H. Johnston and B. Klandermans, eds. (London: UCL Press Limited, 1995), 45.

in forms of cultural innovation, voluntary action inspired by altruism – all of these are grounded in this need for identity and desire to help satisfy it."[2]

> **The jump from identifying with a social movement to being prepared to join the structured nature of a formalized co-operative may be an interesting dilemma for this generation.**

This raises important questions as to how an individual can find and engage with a collective that represents their beliefs and ideologies. The jump from identifying with a social movement to being prepared to join the structured nature of a formalized co-operative may be an interesting dilemma for this generation, which is used to fluidity of choice and subsequently behaving ephemerally.

Hunt, Benford, and Snow explore the extensive literature supporting the notion that changes in identity in new social movements reflect broader macro social change.[3] This "macro" change is a constant source of uncertainty and often of concern. How young people finds themselves "feeling" in this sense may lead to a desire to actively involve themselves in a structure to address the uncertainty or concern.

Young people naturally gravitate towards places and people who represent their sense of "self." It is commonly accepted that the notion of belonging holds a lot of meaning to young people who are developing a sense of identity and structural meaning for their futures. Questions being asked by the co-operative movement in Australia are: How are co-operatives relevant to young people? Are they aware of co-operatives and their potential to formulate and create a sense of belonging and 'self'? What kinds of co-operatives might young people gravitate towards?

> **Young people are in an excellent position to counteract the pure "for profit" market and some of its questionable ethical practices.**

The 2003 Australian Survey of Social Attitudes indicates that 58 per cent of Generation Xers (born between 1969 and 1985) believe that "co-operatives show that people can still work together," while only about 30 per cent believe co-operatives to be old fashioned. There is also a suggestion that one of the major factors influencing this belief is the nature of Generation Xers to "express a desire for unions to have more power…and for the mass media to have less power."[4] A prime example of this: many Generation Xers support environmental social movements as they learn about the un-sustainability of development; they are increasingly aware of the ways in which "modernization and globalization as progress" are causing long-term harm to the environment and threatening the survival of many species.[5]

---

2   Ibid., 49.
3   S.A. Hunt, R.D. Benford, and D.A. Snow, "Identity fields: Framing processes and the social construction of movement identities," in *New social movements: From ideology to identity,* E. Larana, H. Johnston, and J.R. Gusfield, eds. (Philadelphia: Temple University Press,1994), 188.
4   2003 Australian Survey of Social Attitudes.
5   *Adbusters,* 30 (June/July 2000), 60-65

Following from this, young people are in an excellent position to counteract the pure "'for profit" market and some of its questionable ethical practices. Historically, the co-operative movement is dotted with different types of people who were unhappy about being exploited within the capitalist context. Similar attitudes and issues seem to exist today, though now they are not confined to work and health; they have encroached upon our daily intake of food. The Genetically Modified (GM) products appearing at an increasing rate are generating not only protests from activist but also from "boutique" food co-operatives specializing in organic food products – not surprisingly housed within many University Food Co-ops.

Young people are aware of both positive and negative developments within consumer markets. They also possess underlying suspicions concerning what they do not know, as they have become accustomed to being lied to or having information concealed by large companies and governments…only to have details controversially revealed at a later date.

This creates interest to see if they take this feeling and information as a cue to join or start co-operatives that promote openness and democratic decision-making. Will youth who are members of the university food co-ops continue going to the campus after graduation to do their

> Young people are aware of both positive and negative developments within consumer markets.

grocery shopping? Will they set up larger food co-ops closer to where they live or work to be shared by a wider community of people? They have resources and skills – Australia being a fairly free and opportunist country – to develop their own comfortable niches in which to exist and share with others having like-minded concerns.

Young people in Australia now have many options in terms of how they choose to live their lives and participate in areas of particular interest or concern. Generally, young people are not as affected by class or educational issues as generations past, and they have been raised to be choosy about what can benefit them and why. Gen Xers are notorious for mixing and matching belief systems, sub cultures and career moves. This appears to be fertile ground for the establishment of new co-operatives that will serve tailor-made purposes for groups of young people seeking innovation and individuality. Such co-operatives would lend themselves more to interest or recreational pursuits: for example, urban visual artists in Sydney have found forming collectives addresses their creative needs better than trying to "break into" a competitive and sponsored market. They claim to form collectives for both financial and philosophical reasons – tying into the reaction against the biased and often unrepresentative nature of the mass market.

Admittedly, these questions relate largely to young people residing in urban areas where there is more exposure to social movements. Particularly in urban centres, slogans and street press are available everywhere to inform and encourage all locals to engage in positive social, financial and environmental balance. The question now raised is: do Australian youth have sufficient knowledge of the co-operative structure to recognize its potential for creation, fairness and local control? If the answer (as we suspect) is no, how does the movement reach out to this group and guide them in?

These questions can only be answered with more research to help us find new examples and trends, greater dissemination of the information we do know and what we can find out through trial and error "on the ground". If people believe in a concept or cause, they appreciate alternatives, choice and representative structures to engage in meaningfully. Environmental sustainability, organic food, forums to produce and show cultural activities on a local level, freedom from mass market influences, may be a way that the co-operative structure can formally take individuals a step out of identifying with social movement ideology, and engage them in acting collectively, attaining a sense of identity, involvement and achievement in the future.

> These questions can only be answered with more research to help us find new examples and trends, greater dissemination of the information we do know and what we can find out through trial and error "on the ground".

Clarissa Trampe is a graduate in Co-operative Studies from the Polytechnic University of the Philippines. From 1996 to 2001 she served as Officer-In-Charge of the Co-operatives and Livelihood Desk in the Office of Senator Magsaysay, who chaired the Senate Committee on Co-operatives. From 2002 to 2004, she was Youth Co-ordinator for NATCCO, during which time she developed the Co-op Youth Planet Programme. Currently, she is the Marketing Officer for the Metro South Cooperative Bank, a national co-operative bank organized, owned and controlled by co-operatives in the Philippines.

Clarissa S. Trampe,
Philippines

3

When

HANDS ARE HELD TIGHT

A Story of the Endearing People of Claveria

Clarissa S. Trampe

Everything was still dark. Not a streak of sunlight had touched the silent sky. We packed our suitcases and a few days' supply of food and water in the bus. "It would be a long day on the road," my old pals told me. We had to hurry.

In less than an hour, we were outside Manila traversing the North Luzon highway. Daylight started to peek. The dark blue sky slowly changed to red then to yellow, touching everything on earth with the magic of its colours. A few hours later, a surge of excitement enveloped me as I began to see the quiet beauty of our country – a kaleidoscope of cities, rice fields, trees, mountains, bridges, coastal towns, shores and seas.

> a surge of excitement enveloped me as I began to see the quiet beauty of our country – a kaleidoscope of cities, rice fields, trees, mountains, bridges, coastal towns, shores and seas.

We made a few stops to take some food and freshen up a bit.
As we pushed on, the late afternoon sun started to climb down the mountains. Dusk

set in, but we were still on the road. I wondered where we were heading. I had never been there.

It was in June 1997, I was twenty-two. My pals and I were on a mission to evaluate the performance of the Claveria Agri-Based Multi-Purpose Co-operative (CABMPC) as it competed with other co-ops in the Gawad PITAK (Gawad sa Pinakatanging Kooperatiba) in the annual search for the most outstanding co-operative, a contest sponsored by the Land Bank of the Philippines.

> It was also time for me to discover the marvels of the little children who sparked hope in their rather listless community.

"We're here!" exclaimed one of my pals. At last! After 14 hours of travel from Manila, we had reached Claveria, Cagayan, a coastal community on the northwestern tip of the island of Luzon, 740 kilometres from Manila. "Sand!", I felt it as I jumped off from the coaster. I realized that from where we were standing, open water was just two hundred feet away. It's where the Pacific Ocean meets the South China Sea!

The pretty white buildings and the satellite dishes of CABMPC greeted us. The local people welcomed us warmly and served us mouth-watering seafood dishes for dinner. After the great meal, we started to work. We finished late and had to continue the next day. After talking to many people, browsing through a lot of documents and visiting various projects, we concluded the evaluation and headed for another destination.

Within the limited time we had, I learned that CABMPC played a major role in the community of Claveria and the nearby municipalities. But it took me more years and more opportunities of returning annually to this place to really see how the people of Claveria provided the context that allowed CABMPC to become the institution that I found it to be. It was also time for me to discover the marvels of the little children who sparked hope in their rather listless community. One founded on need and fortified by perseverance and discipline. Now that I'm twenty-nine, I know that I cannot talk about CABMPC without talking about Claveria, its history, its people, its community.

Claveria, a Quiet Community

Claveria is a 4th class municipality,[1] blessed with mountains, farms, and seas. About 28,000 people inhabit the place; 13,000 of them are registered voters.[2] A great number of its people depend on farming and fishing. Others go abroad to make a living, while some are employed in government offices.

For many years, Claveria has remained a quiet community. No recreation, aside from what nature offers, exists in Claveria. The children go to school. The folks go to the

---

1 Based on Local Government Code of the Philippines.
2 Data as of 2002. Source: Office of Mayor Pablo Bolante, Jr.

THE AUTHOR (IN RED) AND PALS DURING AN INTERVIEW WITH THE TEACHER-IN-CHARGE OF CLAVERIA EAST CENTRAL SCHOOL.

river or to the sea, to the farms, or to the offices. The day ends when dusk falls and the entire community settles at home.

People marry at a young age, especially those teenagers who cannot go to the cities to pursue a degree since education in Claveria only goes to the secondary school level.

No bank existed in the area until the Rural Bank of Claveria was put up in the 1980s. Before that it would take about four hours to reach the nearest banks in the cities of Laoag or Tuguegarao.

More than three decades ago, there was the Taggat Industries, a logging company nested in the barrio of Taggat and it had employed about 2,000 workers. During its prosperous days, the company provided for the needs of the workers and their families. When the company folded up in the early 80s, people lost their jobs; their families got hungry and scared.

There were not many big businesses in Claveria. There were no livelihood opportunities[and] no available capital except the money from usurers. Some men

EPP STUDENTS AND TEACHER-IN-CHARGE SERVING SCHOOL CHILDREN DURING RECESS AT THE CLAVERIA EAST CENTRAL SCHOOL.

were forced to loot in order to feed their families. Life was difficult for most Claverianos at that time.

Co-ops to the Rescue

Something had to be done. Life could not continue in that way anymore.

The idea of a retired nurse, Mrs. Petra Aguinaldo, seemed to spark hope. She encouraged a small group of people to start what was known as a consumers association. They put up a store and began selling goods to members at a relatively lower price than what was sold by the other traders. They operated their store according to the principles of the co-operative movement. In a short period of time, more people got interested and joined the association which would later be named Claveria Grassroots Mart, Inc.[3]

In 1986 the officers of the Grassroots Mart encouraged the members to put in more share capital so the store could start up a lending operation. The year after, it was

3 Later named Claveria Grassroots Multi-Purpose Co-operative

separated from the consumers operation, which gave way to the establishment of what would be known as the Claveria Agri-based Multi-Purpose Co-operative. Its membership was extended to the neighbouring municipalities of Sanchez Mira and Sta. Praxedes.

The Assistant Manager of the Grassroots Mart, Mrs. Petra Martinez, served as the Manager of CABMPC. With 58,000 pesos, the co-operative began financing the various economic activities of the small vendors, entrepreneurs, farmers and fishermen in the area. Through the co-operative, irrigation facilities were constructed for the farmers. Fish cages and an ice plant were built for the fishermen. They put up a consumers' store, a warehouse, a canteen, a hostel, and a calling centre. They bought the exclusive franchise for cable television in the area.

CABMPC existed without a collection agent, yet were able to collect 95 per cent of its loans through voluntary payment.

In 2000 and 2001, CABMPC bagged the first prize[4] in the Gawad PITAK[5]. These services and more are offered to their 13,000 members who raised the total assets of the co-op to more than three hundred million pesos[6].

Fashioning the Heritage of the Youth

In a land where transportation and communication were once difficult, it's a blessing that a book landed in the hands of Mrs. Martinez; one which gave her bright ideas to tap into one of Claveria's rich resources – the youth.

Being the Guidance Counsellor in the district and at the same time President of the Claveria Teachers' Association for more than 15 years, Mrs. Martinez knew that one of the problems of school children[7] was the lack of variety in healthy foods served at the school canteens. The children were forced to buy from vendors outside. This situation left the canteen with little profit at year end. To help both the children and the school, she proposed the organisation of laboratory (laboratory is probably a bad translation) co-operatives by primary school children, co-operatives that would operate their school canteens.

> It's a blessing that a book landed in the hands of Mrs. Martinez; one which gave her bright ideas to tap into one of Claveria's rich resources – the youth.

It was in 1994, during one of the district meetings of teachers, Mrs. Martinez talked to them about her idea. Since almost every teacher in the area was a member of the CABMC, they readily agreed to it. Point persons were identified. Together, they came

---

4 Five hundred thousand pesos (P500,000.000) worth of fixed assets.
5 The Land Bank of the Philippines honors the country's top bank-assisted cooperatives at its annual Gawad sa Pinakatanging Kooperatiba (Gawad PITAK) awards ceremony at Malacañang Palace.
6 Data as of November 2004. Source: CABMPC General Manager, Mrs. Petra Martinez
7 Generally between the ages 7 to 12, from Grade I to VI

up with plans for its implementation. They would start at the schools nearby, the primary schools of Claveria East Central and the Claveria Central.

General consultations with parents were held to explain to them how it would be done and at the same time secure their approval. This did not present much of a difficulty because the majority of parents were members of CABMPC as well. They, too, supported the creation of the new institution. They agreed that every student would contribute five pesos (P5.00) as share capital, to be given upon entry to the school. This amount, plus the patronage refund, would be given back to the student upon graduation or withdrawal.

The laboratory co-operatives in both Claveria East Central and Claveria Central Schools were then registered under the Co-operative Development Authority[8], with CABMPC serving as their mother co-operative.

SOME OF THE YES CLUB MEMBERS IN
THE CLAVERIA CENTRAL SCHOOL.

The Pupils' Government Organisation (PGO), a representative body of students elected commonly among students in Grades V and VI (about eleven or twelve years old) concurrently served as the officers of the laboratory co-operative. They worked hand-in-hand with the teacher-in-charge in managing the school canteen.

With the capital at hand, they purchased some utensils and simple equipment. They procured the goods from the consumers' store of CABMPC on a consignment basis.

---

8 Created under Republic Act 6939, a government body tasked to register and regulate co-operatives in the Philippines

Parents supplied the other goods. The teacher-in-charge saw to it that the foods were clean and healthy for the children.

A system was devised to ensure that operating the school canteen would not impede on the studies of the children. Students in Grades V and VI were to help out in the canteen during their class hour on EPP[9] (Edukasyong Pantahanan at Pangkabuhayan). All EPP classes were divided into *families* with about 6-8 students in each. For one whole week during the school year, a family would be assigned to the canteen. The members of the family would perform the tasks of cleaning the canteen, preparing the food, listing the sales, counting the money and turning it over to the teacher-in-charge. On occasions, when the school children were busy and could not keep up with their activities in the canteen, the parents would volunteer to assist them.

On the other hand, the school officials made sure that the schedule of recess time for all grade levels was staggered and co-ordinated with the canteen.

> All EPP classes were divided into *families* with about 6-8 students in each. For one whole week during the school year, a family would be assigned to the canteen. The members of the family would perform the tasks of cleaning the canteen, preparing the food, listing the sales, counting the money and turning it over to the teacher-in-charge.

When I visited, I was amazed to witness how the school children in Claveria behaved, especially during recess hours. One section at a time, the students in single file would proceed toward the canteen, each file led by its own leader. Without breaking their queue, they would get their stuff one by one and pay at the counter near the exit. In Claveria Central School, where self-service is employed, the children simply drop their payment at the box before they leave. Then they would head back to their rooms silently and orderly. Truly, it's discipline at its finest! It was a way students learned how to work together, to treat each other with respect, and to behave honestly.

The cycle continued until year end. Although revenues and incomes were computed on a monthly basis, the net proceeds were determined and allotted at the end of the school year, according to this breakdown:

        50 per cent - patronage refund
        20 per cent - school improvements
        15 per cent - canteen improvements
        10 per cent - school reserve fund
         5 per cent - education and training fund
        100 per cent Net Proceeds

Much to the children's delight, the years of operation had given them yearly patronage refunds ranging from 500 per cent to 1000 per cent. There was also a steady supply of funds to support necessary school improvements and programmess such as feeding and participating in inter-school academic competitions.

---

9 Equivalent to Home Economics

Aside from "this" or "the financial benefits", learning the principles and values of co-operatives became fun, easy, and authentic by having the laboratory co-operatives around. Teachers use the co-operative as a reference in teaching Mathematics, Values, English, Language, and other subjects.

The Coins that Changed a Community [10]

An organized group of 4,000 school children gathered coins to raise funds and help their co-operative put up a million-peso calling centre to connect their community to the rest of the world.

They were the wonderful Young Entrepreneurs and Savers (YES) Club members, the schoolchildren who fulfilled the dream of the Claverianos to have in-coming and outgoing telephone access.

The transformation was again led by the vision of CAPBMPC manager, Mrs. Petra Martinez. During the summer of 1999, she noticed that there were plenty of 25-centavo coins scattered around the school grounds, streets, or even in the houses in Claveria. It was evident that the value of money had gone down even in the eyes of the children. "Children did not consider 25 centavo as money anymore. They thought of it as a plaything. If you gave them 25 centavo, they would even cry," said Mrs. Martinez.

The manager felt that something had to be done about the situation. She requested the employees of CABMPC to pick every 25-centavo coin that they saw lying around and bring the coins to the office. They cleaned the dirty coins and bundled them into fours after working hours. It was a comic tale when she presented five boxes of these coins to the Board of Directors. They teased her, asking whether the coins were the per diem they would receive after the meeting.

> She had faith that encouraging schoolchildren to deposit their coins in the co-op would teach them to save money, hence, develop in them the value of thrift.

"With this bundle, you could buy something already." Mrs. Martinez realized that the government had spent money to mint these coins. She had faith that encouraging schoolchildren to deposit their coins in the co-op would teach them to save money, hence, develop in them the value of thrift.

Through the massive campaign of the Education Committee and other officers of the co-op, the YES Club was launched in June 1999 in different elementary and high schools in Claveria and in the neighboring municipality of Sta. Praxedes. Soon after, the club membership was opened to children within the age range of 0-18 years, to include others who also became interested.

---

10 The original transcription was published by the NATCCO Network through The Philippine Coop Sector, Volume 4 No. 1, February 2002, Manila, Philippines.

THE TEACHER AND A PARENT HELPING OUT IN
THE CANTEEN DURING A SCHOOL AFFAIR.

Again, it had not been difficult for
them to start off the YES operation since CABMPC had
proven its competence and commitment in establishing the laboratory co-operatives
in the schools.

Co-ordination with parents and school officials also took place. Children were taught
how to open savings accounts and fill-up deposit or withdrawal slips.

In six months, they were able to amass six million pesos (P6,000,000.00), which
became the co-op's source of funds when it put up the calling centre in February 2000.
To this day, the calling centre generates income for the co-op and connects families
and friends anywhere in the world – an experience the Claverianos were deprived of
for many years.

Today, the YES Club members total 5,600 and their savings deposits amount to
fourteen million pesos (P14,000,000.00).[11]

Every year, during the Co-op Month celebration, the folks watch with delight as
thousands of children parade in the community. They happily show the people how
they are taking care of their future and saving their way to the land of their dreams.

Paying Tribute to the Silent Heroes

The success of the laboratory co-operatives and the YES Club would not have been
possible without the persistent support of teachers who served as extensions of the co-

---

11 Data as of November 2004. Source: CABMPC General Manager, Mrs. Petra Martinez.

op – collecting, recording, and safekeeping the money of the children without getting paid in return. They were indeed exemplary!

The parents, who supported their children's participation in the YES Club activities and assisted in the canteens, are also worth commending.

Being members of CABPMC themselves, they trust that the co-op is strong and stable and that its management is composed of credible, trustworthy and capable people, who would not let them down.

It was not mere luck that brought success to this community. It took the concerted efforts of every member to find solutions to its difficulties.

They say, "It takes a community to raise a child." Yes, it is true. It might be equally true to say that, "It takes children to build a community." They are valuable resources and they have a lot to offer to us.

I was at first charmed by Claveria's serenity, by its mountains, farms, and seas. But spending more of my time with the Claverianos taught me a lot more than I ever expected to find. Here lives a different kind of people – a community that truly thrives on trust, unity and co-operation – and involves its young people in doing so.

THE AUTHOR (IN WHITE) DURING HER THIRD VISIT TO CABMPC, TOGETHER WITH THE GAWAD PITAK EVALUATING TEAM.

4

Chelsea Lake, Canada
Chelsea Lake has worked with the British Columbia Co-oertive Association, attends co-op conferences, and has run workshops at Camp Rainbow, a co-operative youth camp.

THE POWER OF Co-operation

Chelsea Lake

When I was 14 years old I lived on Hornby Island, which is situated off the coast of Vancouver Island, on the west coast of Canada. My early childhood had been very exciting. My parents and I had spent the first six years of my life travelling the world, primarily between Québec, Canada, and India. It was not until I was nine that my family settled down on Hornby.

My parents were pleased to live on a small, peaceful Gulf Island known for its artists, activists and hippies. To them it was a chance to connect with people who shared their values. I could appreciate this but, unlike myself, the kids on Hornby did not seem to share their parents' values. At 14 years old, I needed to find individuals with the same energy, idealism and love for life that consumed me. I needed to be part of something productive, meaningful and fun.

> **I needed to be part of something productive, meaningful and fun.**

Hornby relies on co-operative business to meet much of its economic and community needs. With only 900 residents, it is important for the community to be involved in the decisions of the island's major businesses. It was through the Hornby Island Co-op store that I was able to take part in an experience that would change my life.

In July of 1999, with two other Hornby teenagers and 40 other youth from across British Columbia, I attended Camp Rainbow's Basic Camp. Camp Rainbow is jointly administered by the Rainbow Youth Excellence Society and the BC Co-operative

Association. It runs with support from the co-op and credit union movement in BC and has done so for over 25 years.

Imagine, 55 fourteen and fifteen year olds from all different socio-economic, ethnic, and cultural backgrounds meeting each other for the first time. Kids who got kicked around in high school deliberately paired with kids who kicked others around, city slickers, farm dwellers, suburban mall rats and small town country folk all trying to find common ground. We sat in small groups, mostly with people we already knew, or had somehow forged a connection with, and chatted quietly. As we eyed each other with discomfort and excitement, a camp counsellor armed with a flip chart and smelly markers approached the front of the room. In a clear and serious voice he asked, "What do you want to leave behind this week?"

This question, "What do you want to leave behind this week?" inevitably yields the same answers from every group of teenagers at every camp. By the time a list is fully compiled it includes a range of behaviours and concepts from swearing and put-downs, to disrespect and "isms". "What do you want more of this week?" results in a list that includes sleep and fun, but also inclusion and honesty. Year after year, the same answers emerge, and year after year a large group of teenagers commit to creating an environment of mutual respect and acceptance.

> Imagine, 55 fourteen and fifteen year olds from all different socio-economic, ethnic, and cultural backgrounds meeting each other for the first time.

On my first night of camp, I experienced my first "Reflections". In an activity group of eight or nine people, including two staff members, we met in a small wooden cabin lit only with a candle. After everyone agreed to maintain the confidence of the group by not sharing others' stories outside of the circle, staff members asked the group questions about their lives. One by one participants were asked to share. I had never been asked what my biggest fear was, or who was the most important person in my life. I remember how powerful it was to hear stories I could relate to closely from a group of people I barely knew. It was amazing to me that others shared my insecurities, as well as my need to connect with others. "Reflections" became my favourite time of the day.

Each day, after breakfast there would be a staff-run, interactive session, based on themes of Self-Awareness, Communication, Co-operation and Leadership. These two hour sessions were designed to develop participants' life skills and to bring together the camp community. The co-operation session gave participants a brief background of the co-op movement, and led them through co-operative activities and games. These demonstrated instances when co-operation was more beneficial than competition.

For me, at fourteen, this was an inspirational idea. I had always assumed success was the product of competition. Through competition I would land a good job, lots of money and happiness, or so I was told. By considering co-operation and co-operatives

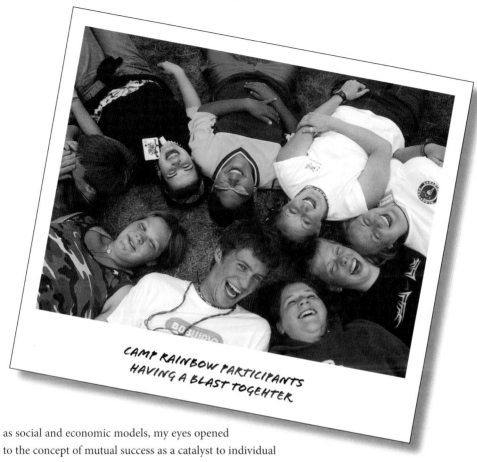

CAMP RAINBOW PARTICIPANTS
HAVING A BLAST TOGEHTER

as social and economic models, my eyes opened
to the concept of mutual success as a catalyst to individual
success. Camp Rainbow introduced me to this idea, and, through the co-operative structure of the camp, I saw first-hand what co-operation could achieve in a community.

Camp Rainbow is unique in that, not only does it have a vibrant and skilled group of facilitators, many of its activities are organized and run by participants. On the first day, campers form committees and choose whether they want to help plan the afternoon activities, the end of the week dance, or work on the general camp environment, among other things. These committees are run co-operatively. Each committee elects two representatives to sit on the town council, which is responsible for relaying information to the community. This resembles a co-operative board of directors. It is democratic and egalitarian. The committees and town council are accountable to the entire community.

> With this experience, knowledge and self-confidence, participants realized that there was tremendous potential to work together to achieve common goals.

As my week at Camp Rainbow progressed, I felt the group of participants grow closer and closer to one another. By the fifth day, people were dreading leaving. Camp Rainbow provided participants with friends for life. The relationships that were forged throughout the week rivalled life-long friendships. For one week we lived in a community where everyone could be herself or himself without fear of rejection or harassment. People opened up to each other and consequently realized that they were not alone. With this experience, knowledge and self-confidence, participants realized that there was tremendous potential to work together to achieve common goals. As people began to realize the power of the experience they had created together, the energy in the camp rose. Participants began to talk about what they wanted in their regular lives, aspects of camp life they didn't want to give up, and components of home life that they didn't want to go back to.

> "The experience I had that summer at Camp Rainbow has helped me realize that I have a vested interest in community development and the co-operative movement.

Returning home from camp was difficult. No one could understand what the experience had meant to me. However, after I had gotten over my initial re-entry shock, I was inspired to use the skills I had gained at camp. My friendships got stronger as I began to encourage honest and open communication. I began to organize activities at school and on the Island. I was suddenly more self-aware and came to understand my true values. My behaviour changed as I tried to live according to my values. I began to really value myself.

I attended the Camp Rainbow Reunion, Advanced Camp and Grad Camp and, when I was sixteen, I joined the staff team. I have been staffing at Camp Rainbow for four years and am committed to helping others have a similar experience to the one that I benefited so greatly from. My life now revolves around ideas of self-development, communication, co-operation and community. I am a political science student in university. The experience I had that summer at Camp Rainbow has helped me realize that I have a vested interest in community development and the co-operative movement.

In a world filled with competition and isolation, I believe it is important to be both accountable to a community and to benefit from its support. I think that co-operatives are an excellent way to achieve this in both rural and urban environments worldwide.

CO-OPERATION IN ACTION

Camp Rainbow is now known as The YES, for more information you can access the YES website at www.theyes.ca, or follow the links on the BCCA website at www.bcca.coop

The main focus of this publication is what young people are contributing to co-operatives today. We are also interested in the lasting impact of such activities, particularly the impact of international young co-operators conferences and other similar sessions.

The following contribution is by two "more experienced youths" in the UK, both of whom can trace their active involvement back to participation in ICA Youth Seminars.

The Editors

Andy Piercy, United Kingdom
Andy Piercy is the General Secretary of the Woodcraft Folk, the national co-operative children's and youth organisation in the United Kingdom.

Mervyn Wilson, United Kingdom
Mervyn Wilson is the Chief Executive and Principal of the Co-operative College in the UK, one of the key organisations in the UK that promote working with young people. The College has actively supported participation in the Co-operative Futures Programmes in Canada, and the ICA Youth Seminars, as well as supporting co-operative youth networks in the UK.

5 WHAT
being involved
as young people
HAS MEANT TO US

1ST ANNUAL BUILDING CO-OPERATIVE FUTURES
YOUTH CONFERENCE, VICTORIA, CANADA, 2003

ANDY LISTENING INTENTLY AT THE BUILDING CO-OP FUTURES YOUTH CONFERENCE, 2003

Andy Piercy

The Woodcraft Folk, along with the Co-operative College in the United Kingdom has actively promoted international work with young people; in particular our recent links with our Canadian partners. The Woodcraft Folk have also played their part in attempting to make the ICA more relevant to young co-operators through active participation in the ICA Youth Seminars.

My own involvement in the co-operative movement has come from the Woodcraft Folk's encouragement of all members over the age of sixteen to become members of their respective co-operative society. I therefore became a member at the first opportunity. I became more active after the merger of my old society with the London Co-operative Society. I was already very active within the Woodcraft Folk, being a member of its General Council.

During the late 60's and early 70's, I attended several international camps in Britain, as well as Western and Eastern Europe, and in 1973 I was one of three Woodcraft Folk members to be nominated to attend the ICA Youth seminar held in Bucharest, Romania.

I became the Woodcraft Folk's international delegate to the two children's and youth international movements and through study visits and exchanges became familiar with the co-operative movement in Poland, Sweden and Portugal.

I became Chair of the area council of the Woodcraft Folk, a body that had both Woodcraft Folk and London Co-operative Society members. Woodcraft Folk members were quite involved in the society, particularly because they were pursuing very progressive policies in terms of peace initiatives during the Cold War period. They also helped the Woodcraft Folk organise fund raising initiatives for medical aid for Vietnam during the Vietnam War.

The Woodcraft Folk had gaps in its international contacts, and we were able to develop exchanges with Portugal, Greece and Poland thanks to Mervyn Wilson, who was then working for the London Co-operative Society. This was to become a long-standing friendship and co-operative relationship spanning several years.

The Woodcraft Folk pioneered contact between children's organisations in Eastern Europe when these were treated with suspicion by the government of the day. We also had difficulty with some sections of the co-operative movement. We held to a vision of a world without frontiers and without divisions between East and West.

The Woodcraft Folk were very aware of the UK's imperial past and it was important for us to develop exchanges with what became countries beyond Europe. In doing so, we came into increasing contact with co-operatives in India, Bangladesh and Latin America. All of these new contacts involved young people and it's true to say the participants' experiences were life changing. Our exchanges with India and Latin America, for example, certainly resulted in members choosing to study international development, international relations or Latin American studies at university.

> What motivates young people are the co-operative movement's ideals and principles and the development of Fair Trade and ethically sourced products.

These positive experiences sometimes contrasted with those in Britain, where the co-operative movement has treated young people as committee fodder. The Woodcraft Folk organised all activities co-operatively, making decisions at its General Council by consensus. It is a world away from dated structures and procedures that we want to change. To this end, I am working positively to encourage greater diversity and participation.

What motivates young people are the co-operative movement's ideals and principles and the development of Fair Trade and ethically sourced products. Working with the Co-operative Group, the motivated young people in the Woodcraft Folk want to extend these concerns to all our purchases wherever possible.

Young people readily understand why we have encouraged Woodcraft Folk members to use the Co-operative Bank, buy from consumer co-operatives, worker co-operatives and socially responsible companies.

They are passionate supporters of initiatives to help develop our work with Palestine through exchanges with its fledgling co-operative movement, a fine example of what motivated me to stay involved both with the Woodcraft Folk and the Co-op.

ROCHDALE 160TH ANNIVERSARY: FROM LEFT, STEPHEN YOUD-THOMAS (THE CO-OPERATIVE GROUP) AND MARK CRAIG (UNITED CO-OPERATIVES) CO-SPONSORED THE EVENT, SEEN HERE WITH IAN MACPHERSON, STEPHEN YEO, MERVYN WILSON, AND CHRIS COOPER.

Mervyn Wilson

My involvement in the co-operative movement came directly as a result of work with young people. I had been active in the student movement, shortly after I graduated and took up a post as organiser of the British delegation to the World Youth Festival, held in East Berlin in 1973. We took over 400 young people from a range of trade unions, the Labour Movement, political, faith-based and young people's organisations.

It was through that work that I gained my contacts with the co-operative movement. It provided us with offices and administrative support, and the education and political wings of the two giant co-operative societies in London supported the project.

Shortly after the project finished, the London Co-op was recruiting an education organiser, and they invited me to apply. They were particularly keen to get someone experienced in working with young people.

About a year after I had joined the London Co-op, they offered me a place on a small British delegation attending the International Co-operative Alliance Youth Seminar in Moscow. In those days the seminars were two-part events – two or three day formal seminars with lots of discussion, in those days particularly on the role

YOUTH REINVENTING CO-OPERATIVES

of the co-operative movement in promoting peace (remember the Vietnam War had barely ended, and the Cold War certainly had not). This was followed by a three day study visit looking at co-operatives in Byelorussia, Lithuania, and on to Leningrad (St Petersburg) in Russia. It was that combination, a chance for open debate with young people actively involved in co-operatives from all over the world, together with a chance to look at different co-operatives, which was so important.

It was during that early period working with the London Co-operative Society that I first met Andy Piercy, who had been at the previous International Co-operative Alliance Youth Conference in Romania. He was one of the dynamic young leaders in the Woodcraft Folk, the children's and youth organisation that is supported by the co-operative movement, and which was particularly strong in the Greater London area.

> The experiences at events such as the Co-operative Futures Forums and other international gatherings are life-changing experiences for the participants involved.

One of the biggest problems we often face is that we look at co-operatives from the narrow perspective of our own direct experience. In the UK that experience is often about consumer co-operation, so having a chance to meet and talk with young people active in agricultural co-operatives, housing co-operatives, student co-operatives, and visiting such co-operatives helps you to realise what a vast international movement you are part of.

Friendships were formed from which other projects developed. In London we ran young co-operators exchanges for many years with strong involvement by young employees. It was from that that we developed work with schools, taking head teachers to study school co-operatives in Poland, years ahead of the mini-enterprise projects in the UK. The other thing that was remarkable was how many of the young people involved in those seminars not only remained in touch for many years to come, but moved in to major positions of responsibility within their movements. Gabriella Sozanski from Hungary, for example, now Head of Knowledge Management at the International Co-operative Alliance, was a delegate to the Moscow Youth Conference, and another delegate headed the International Department of Poland's Supreme Co-operative Council for many years.

All remained highly committed to strategies involving young people in the long-term. They became passionate advocates for young co-operators and international work.

Put simply, the experiences at events such as the Co-operative Futures Forums and other international gatherings are life-changing experiences for the participants involved. That is why I remain deeply committed to them, and will ensure that the Co-operative College continues to work to promote such activities.

The following two interviews, kindly provided to us by the Northeast Federation of Cooperatives (www.cooplife.coop), provide perspectives from two young people who are deeply involved in the American co-operative movement.

Katie Brennan,
United States

Katie Brennan is a member of Impact Visuals, a worker co-operative in New York City.

Jennifer Gutshall,
United States

Jennifer Gutshall is a member of the Connecticut Energy Co-op in Hartford, Connecticut.

6 WHAT
being involved
MEANS TO US

Nicholas Herman interviews Katie Brennan.

NH: Please introduce yourself and describe what you do.

KB: My name is Katie Brennan. I am 24 years old and am a new member on the staff of Impact Visuals. Impact Visuals is a co-operatively owned photography archive and publication service in New York City. Mostly, we provide pictures to different magazines for publication. What is unique about our archives, and the photographers that own and run Impact, is the focus on social justice and multicultural stories. Most of our archives consist of pictures documenting protests, under-represented minority groups, or other socially charged subjects. Because of our focus, many alternative publications such as feminist and environmental magazines use our archives extensively.

NH: How many members are there?

KB: There are approximately 80 member photographers and six staff.

NH: How did you find out about Impact Visuals?

KB: It was really through chance. I discovered them on the Internet and ultimately was able to arrange for an internship. I can't stress enough the importance of internships. Before I did an internship I did not have a good sense of what I could do with my interest in photography. Internships empower young people by giving them responsibility.

NH: Is there a common mission among the co-op members?

KB: Well yes and no. There definitely is a core value of documenting people and their fight for self-determination. Also the goal is to support the photographers who do this kind of work and are members of the co-op. When I started I didn't consider myself an activist or anything. I never really considered myself an activist before coming to Impact, nor did I have any experience with co-operatively owned business. I came to NYC from a small town in Pennsylvania. I grew up in a single-parent family environment and have always been sensitive to the lack of support systems both for working mothers and their kids. The first time I ever really brought my interest in photography and social rights together was during college. I got a BFA from Edinburgh University, which is near Erie, Pennsylvania. We had a final project and I produced a photo documentary of single mothers working in service industry jobs – mostly waiting tables. So I guess the politics and the art and the economics all sort of merge in different ways for the different members.

> I feel like there needs to be more education and exposure – the web is a great vehicle, it worked for me.

NH: What are your job responsibilities?

KB: When I was an intern I began learning about managing the archives which requires a thorough knowledge of what pictures we have and how to quickly find good images that match the needs of the magazines. We have a detailed system of cataloguing more than two million pictures on file – it's a big job! Now that I am on staff, I work in both the archives and with the new interns. I also help manage our accounts with the different magazines and publications that order from Impact Visuals. One example of what I do is this – just yesterday Newsweek emailed a request for pictures illustrating tension between Lebanon and Israel. So first we went to the International file, then to the Israel and Lebanon files, and finally to the War file.

NH: How does being a young person impact your job?

KB: Well, when I began that photo documentary of workers during college I was really responding to my own standing concern for young people and the lack of opportunities they have in rural, low-income environments. So even though I wasn't well versed in cooperative economics I was seeing the connection between workers being exploited and their lack of education and decision making power. So my desire to empower young people, and workers in general, is partly informed by my being young and feeling a connection with their life and my own.

NH: How does being in a co-op affect your job and the work environment?

KB: I feel that there is a big difference working in a co-operatively owned atmosphere. First off, my co-workers really listen to my ideas. There isn't any strict hierarchy and I

YOUTH REINVENTING CO-OPERATIVES

am constantly impressed with the level of communication. Also, I have some creative control over what I choose for publication, I guess I feel that there is a level of trust and respect that I haven't felt in other work environments. The actual work environment reflects a more community-oriented approach as well. There are no cubicles!

NH: How does Impact Visuals, as a co-op, serve its members?

KB: It creates a means of distributing their work, which is probably the most important way. Our member photographers believe strongly in the importance of this kind of photojournalism and Impact Visuals supports this mission. As far as the members' roles, they take part in all the major decisions about how the archive will be maintained. For example, our biggest issue now is how to digitize the archive and make it available online. That will be a huge job but will increase visibility and opportunities for our members to be published.

NH: What are your goals for personal development?

KB: Well I guess I would like to improve my own photography and begin to strengthen my own artistic and political voice as well as better serve under-represented communities. I have struggled a lot with my professional direction and how to represent my community. My job has not only helped me learn skills, it has actually encouraged my desire to represent and serve my community! Although it feels a little awkward to say, I feel like I am becoming a role model for other young artists and activists.

NH: How about your goals for co-op development?

KB: I would love to see more young people being exposed to co-ops and learning about how co-ops can work for them. The lack of awareness is just part of the larger problem I see where many young people don't receive the education and exposure to alternatives that they deserve.

NH: In your opinion how could co-ops better attract and include young people?

KB: Well partly co-ops need to see young people as a new wave of knowledge and skill sets. I do think we are more technologically literate. Also our concerns are often somewhat different and if a co-op wants to attract young people as customers than it should have young people on its staff. I know that as an employee at Impact Visuals I have a young eye and am often able to see a picture that might be more poignant or powerful to a youth audience. This holds true when I am actually taking the picture as well. I know where to go and what to look for when it comes to representing youth issues. Again, I feel like there needs to be more education and exposure – the web is a great vehicle, it worked for me. I don't think I ever would have found out about Impact Visuals without it.

Nicholas Herman interviews Jennifer Gutshall

NH: Please introduce yourself:

JG: My name is Jennifer Gutshall and I am twenty-eight years old.

NH: When did you get involved in Co-ops?

JG: I didn't get involved in co-ops until 1996 when I moved to Connecticut – I don't think I even really had a concept about co-ops in college. I started to get involved with a number of groups who were advocating alternative economic systems, such a barter system where we used "community dollars". There I was informally exposed to the concept of co-operatives and more specifically the energy co-op.

NH: What is an energy co-op?

JG: An energy co-op is a consumer co-operative that provides energy – be it electricity, oil, propane, or conservation and efficiency services. We try to provide the spectrum of energy services with an increasing emphasis on renewable energy sources.

NH: Let's back up, whom do you work for and how did you get started there?

JG: I work for the Connecticut Energy Co-op. My boss is Larry Union, the general manager and CEO who works for the board of directors of CEC. Our board is made up of a diverse group of interests from across Connecticut – from neighbourhood groups to national organizations like the Sierra Club. Basically, anyone who is interested in democratic alternative energy structures where the goal is meeting peoples' energy needs in a more affordable, environmental, and democratic way.

NH: That sounds like your mission statement!

JG: It is close. Our mission statement is: The Connecticut Energy Co-op was organized to create and maintain an environmental, social and economically sustainable future rooted in Connecticut and responsive to the needs of its members.

NH: Are the staff members of the co-op?

JG: Definitely! We are all totally committed to this cause.

NH: Jennifer you have mentioned that the success of the C.E.C. was largely due to the type of organizing that you did at the outset. Can you explain what that entailed?

JG: You can look at it in stages. The only thing that has made it possible for the co-op to exist as it does now is the support of the diverse group of community leaders and organizations that got involved at the conception. This diverse constituency has given our co-op a dynamic basis on which to grow. Before we started we wanted to insure that we had a viable market. In order to do this we began assessing the needs and desires of the people of Connecticut. It is interesting what happened. There were inevitably disagreements about what kind of energy we should provide. One of the primary issues was whether or not to provide dirty energy; i.e. energy based on fossil fuels. So the co-op had to struggle with the ideals of energy conservation versus the requisite energy needs of the community. We decided that we had to get involved with utilities first and then evolve over time to be environmentally cleaner. Jack Northrup of the New Hampshire Consumer Utility Cooperative used to say that you have to build the boat before you steer it. So the process of starting our co-op was a lesson in democracy and economics as well as ideals.

One of the core goals of our cooperative is to help our members use as little energy as possible so as to both save them money and reduce environmental impact. We can measure the success of these goals through our new I.C.E. program. I.C.E. stands for innovation, conservation, and efficiency.

NH: So one of the things that you are offering, indeed, selling, is education and economic savings.

JG: Yes, a very practical way of appealing to people. The fact is that co-ops don't have the traditional profit motive so that we have the latitude to really focus on our larger mission. We provide a free energy audit that can catalyze a conversation about how customers can increase their involvement in savings. We also provide an ongoing context for our members to evolve in their pursuit of conservation and efficiency.

The question really is why don't people who are committed to conservation use the very products that reduce energy consumption, products like compact fluorescent bulbs? In my opinion it is a matter of education.

NH: Are you in the role of an educator at Connecticut Energy Cooperative?

JG: I will be! Right now I am primarily focused on the structures that will give me access to members that in turn will allow me to help provide support and access to their continuing education. Once these structures are in place, the ball really gets rolling. Once the members know what they want, then we in turn must be able to provide the products and services that they request, in addition to financing so that they can afford these services. Clean energy should not only be available to the wealthy.

NH: What do you do, specifically, at C.E.C.?

JG: Well I am the manager of Member Services. This means that on the one hand I manage all aspects of customer services, i.e. providing all levels from enrolment to fulfillment. Any customer questions, concerns, complaints are directed at me. Right now, as I have said, the emphasis is on customer service – making sure they are getting their needs met. When we have built a strong customer base, then my role will shift and I will be more focused on education.

NH: Jennifer how does C.E.C. plan to appeal to young adults?

JG: I would say that the primary way that we reach that market is through the message that we are sending. My hope is that college-aged people and young adults will be attracted to both our offering of savings and energy efficiency. One of the programs that we have gotten directly involved in is this year's Earth Day. Once we have gotten past the initial stage of start-up, I would like to emphasize our number of new programs that would directly appeal to young people. One of these programs would be to work with Solar Works. Solar Works is one of the primary initiatives behind the Solar on School Program. This school program is a regional effort to bring solar electricity into the schools. There are also a number of Universities such as Tufts where there is an increasing desire to implement Eco-friendly practices on an institutional level. Tufts have actually committed to begin to honour the Kyoto standards for air emissions. So one of the possibilities for our energy co-op would be to build strategic relationships with committed educational and religious institutions – often these institutions have a mission that includes values of stewardship or increasing the value of life. Obviously, if a group is committed to quality of life they can't ignore the quality of the environment.

NH: I want to ask you if you feel that there are any limitations of the co-operative approach.

JG: I don't believe that there are any limitations to people working together for positive change and innovation. My motto is garbage in garbage out. If we remain positive there is no limitation to human connection and human power. There is a leap of faith when co-ops mobilize and move to revolutionize business practices. In the energy sector we are up against a dinosaur. There are challenges certainly, and ours is an alternative vehicle, but I have first hand experienced that when people work together they really can mobilize and change policy. The fact is that our concepts of space and time are changing so rapidly as a result of travel and technology that the real power is even more in the hands of the individual – that person who makes a lifestyle or value decision to act. If we don't empower ourselves in this way then we risk getting dragged by the current of change.

The energy industry is inherently conservative, a real old boys' network and there are definitely problems with the old ways of thinking. The fact is that we fight wars to protect our fossil fuel interests. One way to look at the challenges confronting cooperative and alternative energy is not to be overwhelmed by what is wrong but stay focused on what we are doing that is progressive and right. Together we can join, push out, and transform the community. I really feel that the ideas we promote though our co-operative organization are beginning to educate the public about viable alternatives. The change is palpable.

NH: Why are young people important?

JG: Young people have so much more flexibility than most older people do. They are in a rare position to dramatically change the status quo – something we desperately need. They are the leaders of the future after all. But more pragmatically, young people who are committed to social and environmental change will learn quickly that real change requires long-term investment. But this is why young people are essential – we need the next generation to begin to turn back the previous centuries of selfish profit motivated gain – in short, we need some radical youth energy!

NH: What are your personal goals and vision for the future?

> I really believe that when people have access to education that they will make the right choice!

JG: My primary long-term interest is creating self-sustainable communities. Now obviously there are different definitions for what communities represent, but I believe that the future is in building inter and intra dependent communities that are working from basic values of environmental sustainability and human needs. This is a bioregional approach and one that is heavily based on working democratic ideals and continuing education. Co-ops are the perfect structures to begin to build these relationships because they are inherently democratic and are not profit driven. I really believe that when people have access to education that they will make the right choice!

Mirta Vuotto,
Argentina

Mirta Vuotto is a member of the Faculty of Economic Sciences. University of Buenos Aires. Vice-chair South America ICA Committee on Co-operative Research (ICACCR).

What do young university students think about WORKING IN CO-OPERATIVES?

Mirta Vuotto

Introduction

Hoping to stimulate student interest within the professional cycle of the Faculty of Economic Science at the University of Buenos Aires, we undertook a study to determine how students perceived working in a co-operative venture[1]. In conducting

---

1   The University of Buenos Aires (UBA) is a public university founded in 1821. It is the largest university in the country and according to census data from 2000 the enrolment was: 254,260 undergraduate and 8,809 graduate students, 5,555 students in intermediate levels and 17,237 students of UBA XXI (externals). There are 24,835 faculty (70 per cent regular and 30 per cent ad-Honorem). In the Faculty of Economic Sciences there are 41,073 students enrolled in the degrees of Actuary, Administrartion, National Public Accounting, Economy, and Information Systems. It is the faculty with the largest student

our research, we linked theoretical perspectives concerning the structure and the functioning of different types of organisations to the students' opinion about working in co-operatives[2]. We wanted:

- to understand how they viewed work in those ventures; and
- to investigate what kind of organisation they would wish to join when they completed their degrees.

In essence, this study is an analysis of opinions: that is, of the attitudes or judgments people form about something in question, in this case the opinions of young people on working in co-operatives. We define "opinions" as a reflection of "what people think" or "what they believe"; they represent a person's mental disposition when they are asked to respond to various situations and questions. They can be based on values, on relatively stable beliefs, on convictions, or occasional circumstances through which people pick up or represent elements of social reality; they emerge from owned or shared observations and experiences.[3]

The study's data is the result of a survey done among 497 students enrolled in the course *Sociology of Organisations* in the year 2004.

Methodology

We used a questionnaire containing three sections: the first was made up of a grid in which we gathered information on the students' basic socio-demographic characteristics, focusing on their life as students and on their working experience. The second section of the questionnaire examined the way they visualized work in co-operative ventures. This included the recruitment of personnel and their incorporation, their training and their compensation. In the third section, we investigated students' preferences for future professional placements and the reasons why they made their choices.

The issues related to working in co-operatives were identified in keeping with the approach common in human resources texts,[4] and it was gathered through interviews with key informants. This information was used to design the closed questions of the final survey.

---

body (16.2 per cent) and according to the teaching census of 2000, there are 1,903 faculty, 1,767 are professors and the rest are assistants.

2   The contents are part of the programme curriculum for the subject "Sociology of Organisations" which is taught in the professional cycle for the degrees in Administration and Systems in the Faculty of Economic Sciences at UBA.

3   P. Abramson, *Political Attitudes in America* (San Francisco: Freeman and Co, 1983).

4   See C. Cooper, ed., *Fundamentals of Organisational Behavior*, Four-Volume Set (London: Sage, 1996); C. Huxham, ed., Creating Collaborative Advantage. (London: Sage, 1996); A. Sagie and M. Koslowsky, Participation and Empowerment in Organisations: Modelling, Effectiveness, and Applications (London: Sage, 1999).

The survey tool was a 24-question questionnaire (21 closed and 3 open). Following a pre-test, we formulated specific questions on co-operative ventures. We used a Likert type scale (5 showing maximum agreement and 1 minimum) to measure responses.

The open questions were used to analyse the choices students would make when they selected the type of organisation in which they would like to be placed after they completed their studies. We were particularly interested in the reasons they chose for supporting their decision.

Analysis of the results

To conduct the analysis of the descriptive questions of the sampled population, we proceeded with the usual technique of variable construction, starting from the encoding of several questions. In the case of the answers to the open questions, related to the choice of organisation and their motives, we systematised the analysis using two procedures:

- the construction of categories to codify and extract frequency of answers; and
- the organisation of the ideas evident within the context of the answers.

The population

The population under study was made up of 497 students[5] enrolled in Business Administration (468) and Information Systems (27). For both degrees, a course in Sociology of Organisations is mandatory. For the remaining students, those taking degrees in Public Accounting, Court Clerking and Economics (15), this sociology course in an elective.

The ratio of males to females was 96.4 (number of males per 100 females). The distribution was as follows:

Interviewed students

Socio-demographic characteristics	Work		Do not work		Total
Gender Age group	Fem.	Masc.	Fem.	Masc.	
20 - 25	123	138	103	55	419
26 - 29	17	34	4	1	56
30 and over	4	14	2	2	22
	144	186	109	58	497

---

5   13 students out of the 497 were enrolled both in Public Accounting and Business Administration degrees at the same time.

Of those polled, 60.5 per cent were admitted into the faculty between the years 2001 and 2002 and 67.3 per cent had successfully passed between 11 and 15 subjects in their degree programme.

Within the sample, 66.4 per cent of the student's presently work. The majority (226) do so in business organisations, among which the INC. and the LTD. are dominant. The remainder of the participants work in sole proprietorship business (50), self-employed (20), or in public administration (28). Only one of the students works in a co-operative venture.

The tasks they performed in those working areas were mostly administrative (41.6 per cent). They are followed in importance by marketing activities (16.9 per cent) and duties linked to computer science and production.

How do they view working in a co-operative?

The topics the students were asked about were linked to working in co-operatives; procedures used in recruiting and incorporating personnel; training activities, and the nature of workers' compensation.

The formulated questions concerning the first topic refer to the nature of the job and the range of tasks. Here we investigated the worker's degree of autonomy relative to the execution of the job (task sequence, methods, tools, etc.); to the time of work (rhythm, breaks, schedules, etc.); and to the work organisation itself (objectives, norms, etc.). The goal was to differentiate strategic extrinsic attributes (salary, schedules, social benefits, working conditions) from intrinsic or expressive attributes that make work itself a source of satisfaction (use of abilities, responsibility, recognition, etc.). This way, students were asked to evaluate the work according to the resources it implicitly uses and what it contributes to the individual. They also had to consider the co-operative organisation's functional structure from the point of view of the roles played by its members.

The students' responses supported the view that, when it comes to co-operatives, the intrinsic factors are perceived as very positive and help to motivate workers.[6] The students tended to highlight the greater level of autonomy presented in the co-operatives (66.6 per cent) and emphasized the importance of teamwork and network tasks involved (73.4 per cent). An important agreement was found between the incentives the worker received for taking decisions (59.6 per cent) and the rotation of tasks that are considered typical for these organisations (52.2 per cent).

The diversity of tasks included in the work in a co-operative was perceived as a unique characteristic of these organisations by 69 per cent of the students. They also underlined the importance of being able to help incorporate changes into the work

---

6   F. Herzberg, *Work and the Nature of Man* (New York: Crowell, 1966).

they performed. This variable usually translated into intrinsic gratification for the job itself, inasmuch as it allowed options or a degree of freedom relative to methods and work schedules, as well as to quality criteria on the worker's side. Just as the lack of variety that makes a job easily programmable can alienate the employee from the work process, it is widely documented that variety increases worker satisfaction.[7]

The second part of the survey considered the processes of personnel incorporation in the co-operatives. In this area we need to acknowledge the lack of information about numerous issues related to the resources and techniques used in the selection and recruitment of workers. Nevertheless, students did express opinions. Their responses indicate that the workers' capacity in collaborating and working in a team within co-operatives is taken into account (75 per cent) and their capacity for contributing to the strategic objectives of the venture is valued (69.2 per cent). The tendency to value the employee's potential for learning was recognized by 51.5 per cent of those polled.

> The students' responses supported the view that, when it comes to co-operatives, the intrinsic factors are perceived as very positive and help to motivate workers.

The third part referred to training activities and contained questions related to the objectives and modalities that these activities present. Similar to the attributes that were highlighted above, the strongest level of agreement occurred around the objectives of such activities as promoting teamwork and interpersonal relationships (71.1 per cent), advancing job positions (53.5 per cent) and expanding on work experiences (58.7 per cent). The answers indicate some lack of understanding concerning the degree of continuity these activities present, as well as the time and money investment that they require and their relationship to the individual's career path.

In examining workers' compensations in the co-operatives, we took into account that the achievement of the workers' co-operation in the collective execution of some common objectives helps define and preserve the permanent equilibrium between each and everyone's contributions and also affects the agreed upon compensation rewards.[8] These rewards differ in nature: they can be tied to the actual nature of the exercised activities (challenge, autonomy, responsibility, risk, etc.); to the possibilities of the social relationships they share (with colleagues, clients, providers, etc.); to the financial or symbolic status they confer (work security, prestige, prerogatives, and various advantages); and to the objectives that they help meet.

---

7   In order to modify or reform unfavourable situations (Savall, 1994) companies can adopt different forms: job rotation, job enlargement and job enrichment. In general these forms are based on phycological assumptions and the lead restructuring task (Guiot, 1985). See J.R. Hackman and G.R. Oldham, "Motivation through the design of work: Test of a theory" *Organisational Behavior and Human Performance*, (1976): 16; N. Leonard, L. Beauvais, and R. Scholl, "Work motivation: The incorporation of self-concept-based processes," *Human Relations*; 52:8 (August 1999); G.R. Salancik and J. Pfeffer, "A social information processing approach to job attitudes and task design," *Administrative Science Quarterly*, (1978): 23.
8   C. Barnard, *The Functions of the Executive* (Cambridge, MA: Harvard University, 1938).

In principle, such rewards are important as workers compare them with the rewards offered by other kinds of venture, including salaries. Put another way, management has many ways in which to encourage employees to enthusiastically support an organisation's objectives. In that regard, financial incentives play an important role, though not enough in themselves to ensure a worker's full engagement in the accomplishment of a common task.

Thus, it can be argued, the worker's perceived intangible compensation not only plays an instrumental role but constitutes a determining factor in the organisation's existence. What is more, it shapes the strategic alignment of the objectives and activities of all groups in the organisation towards a common purpose, its internal equity, external competitiveness, and the quality of people's performance. The perceived intangible compensation is related to the person's type of work, the results that are expected, and, ultimately it affects the remuneration level as well. This exogenous variable is perhaps the best-known predictor of satisfaction because it translates into the daily rewards that indirectly communicate the degree to which the organisation values its employees.

Recognising the importance and the reach of the above-mentioned basic functions in co-operative enterprises, we formulated the questionnaire items relating to the employees' compensation in these organisations. Close to one half of those polled considered that compensation is established according to a formal system, although there was less agreement than expected considering that they all know the system by which it is based. According to most of the respondents, their desired compensation was based more on personal than on economic incentives, meaning that they placed professional career development and recognition above salary issues. Although they also highlight that other benefits are included in the compensation, most of those polled could not specify what the gap was between the workers and administrative employees' compensation and those of managers.

In summary, the shared opinions on the four topics mentioned above reveal that the students' limitations in understanding work in co-operatives in a precise manner lies in the scarce information they had available. They were limited in their knowledge because co-operatives are inadequately studied in the faculty's degree programme.

There are few incentives within the faculty to encourage, produce and disseminate research on the topic and, within the university; it is considered foreign to professional concerns and, in many cases, co-operatives are not visualised as serious business ventures; the different but important aspects of the work that should be included when evaluating their effectiveness are simply avoided. Thus students had difficulty in understanding the unusual aspects of co-operatives as an organisational form as compared with the classic capital enterprise. This is a serious problem because it means that they have not developed within their professional training the practical skills that such ventures require.

The students' preferences

Complementarily, the study focused on the students' potential choices as future professionals for placement in various types of organisations and the reasons for supporting their decision.

In this topic we considered the bilateral character of every recruiting process, in the sense that, just as the enterprise selects the ideal candidate in relation to the characteristics of the post it wishes to cover, the candidates also select the companies that are most attractive to them.[9]

In this respect, the literature on the issue establishes a certain correlation between auto-selective tendencies and the image of the organisation. The auto-selective tendencies are determined by the image that potential members of an organisation form about what is requested and what is offered to them. This image significantly influences the disposition toward being recruited. When the potential member can choose from several organisations, it is assumed that the organisation with the more attractive image will be more attractive for a prospective employee. Such firms will also find it easier to receive from the surrounding world what it needs to function successfully: that is, not only employees, but also clients, capital, incentives, and help.

From this perspective and based on the apparent factors that determined preference, we assumed that students would be most attracted to enterprises offering more lucrative rewards, notably the multinational corporations of great size.

Although 67.0 per cent prefer to be placed in business organisations, within this group 50.1 per cent express their preference for the small and medium sized enterprises, (SMEs) while 16.9 per cent prefer multinational corporations of great size. While 11.1 per cent have not yet decided in what organisation they would like to work, 10.9 per cent would consider working in co-operatives or being self-employed (9.9 per cent). Only 6 of those polled (1.2 per cent) opted for working in the public sector.

> Taken as a whole, the respondents who preferred co-operatives saw them as enterprises that provided particular satisfaction in the areas of ability, extending responsibility and recognition, fostering professional progress, and encouraging personal growth and development.

The small group of students who expressed a preference for working in co-operatives did so for a number of reasons. First and foremost, they valued the work as it contributes to the individual. To support this decision, they primarily referred to the relationships of work with their co-workers and the possibility of developing professionally and personally to obtain experience, to advance themselves professionally, to learn and to acquire knowledge.

---

9   R. Mayntz, *Sociología de la organización* (Madrid: Alianza, 1987).

In addition, they cited reasons that are particular to working in co-operatives. They emphasized that co-ops are often less structured and have a less formal character, that responsibilities are better understood, that the workplace is pleasant, that there is more freedom, and that it fosters constant productivity and improvement.

Taken as a whole, the respondents who preferred co-operatives saw them as enterprises that provided particular satisfaction in the areas of ability, extending responsibility and recognition, fostering professional progress, and encouraging personal growth and development. Clearly, this group of respondents perceives work as a combination of economic income, personal freedom, opportunities for socialization and involvement in an activity that contributes to one's quality of life in general.

In the students' words, "the work grants greater freedom to the employees, who can improve it according to their criteria"; they also said, "through group activities you obtain benefits for the enterprise as you co-operate with others to obtain them" and "the existing participation incentives allows the worker self-fulfillment". Thus the result is that "in the co-operatives the individual is more valued as a person" and therefore they "present greater possibilities to grow and develop professionally", so "economic well-being is achieved simultaneously with professional and personal development."

Conclusion

The attributes and dimensions highlighted by the students as they visualize the work in co-operative enterprises leads us to think about the importance of the equilibrium between 1) the incorporation of organisational values on the side of the employees and 2) the incorporation of organisational priorities, which reflects an economic dimension whose consequences are expressed in the organisation's strategic alignment. This no doubt represents a dimension of a cultural nature whose consequences are translated on the plane of the social implications within the organisation.

As long as the equilibrium is long-lasting, it is possible from an analytical perspective, to differentiate issues, such as the implication, satisfaction and motivation of the workers and to realise that the co-operative enterprise can go beyond its immediate economic objectives to become a place where employees can more fully realise their personal goals.

In this way, the co-operatives' employees will want to channel their energies to improve the quality of work in the organisation, to align themselves with the organisation's priorities, and to spontaneously co-ordinate their own work with that of the team.

8

Erik Haensel, Canada
Erik Haensel is a researcher with the British Columbia Institute for Co-operative Studies and is registered in a History and Environmental Studies programme at the University of Victoria.

A WORLD OF POSSIBILITIES:
Youthful & Useful
Co-operative Information
on the Internet

Erik Haensel

The Internet is like a vast library where keystrokes can scan shelves of books in moments and mouse clicks will propel you through seemingly infinite floors of information. But it is also a confusing maze with masses of information organized in disparate fashion. Embarking on what seems like a quick search can result in hours of frustrated flipping between this page and that, search engines and endless lists of links. Finding information on the Internet can be akin to searching for lost money in the sand.

Yet, the Internet is a potent resource, and over the past few weeks I have found tomes of information about co-operatives from around the world. I have been searching for co-operative information that is relevant to youth in order to help put together a useful nexus or entry point for youth seeking co-operative information on the Internet. Soon, this information will be available in the Cooperative Learning Centre website: www.learningcentre.coop.

As I career through cyberspace I am learning about the enigmatic place of the Internet in our lives. It provides a space for so many different types of engagement. In order to effectively glean information from this resource, we will need to explore and understand the different roles and uses that the Internet is home to.

In the following paragraphs I have reflected upon my own Internet journey, with the hopes of providing a starting place for others, particularly young people, searching for co-operative information.

> If we understand our computers as portals, or doorways, we may understand the complexity of what is possible in virtual media. Just as I can walk through the door of my local library, I can open an online book search.

If we understand our computers as portals, or doorways, we may understand the complexity of what is possible in virtual media. Just as I can walk through the door of my local library, I can open an online book search. By the same token, I may also use the computer portal to enter into a specific subculture, such as that of the UBC Bike Co-op, an experience that is the virtual equivalent of walking through the door into a bustling bike repair shop.

Unlike libraries, computers provide leisure opportunities alongside work, research and information gathering. During my searches for information on youth in co-operatives, I was continually compelled to embark on more playful experiences of interaction with my Internet exploration. Compelled to seek out photographs of far away places, or read reviews of recently released movies, I was beckoned

ERIK WORKING AT THE BRITISH COLUMBIA
INSTITUTE FOR CO-OPERATIVE STUDIES

YOUTH REINVENTING CO-OPERATIVES

towards taking a step in differing directions. Sometimes I did follow these whims, and more often than not found myself suddenly immersed in a totally different experience from which I had considerable difficultly disengaging, let alone finding my way back to the co-op website which I had left. Such diversions are a great risk – or a great pleasure – of research on the Internet…even for the most die-hard co-operative enthusiast.

The usefulness of the Internet, and the path with you should walk down to get what you need, varies based on the type and location of the information that you seek.

For instance, if you were hoping to find information on Student Housing Co-operatives in Canada, you could begin at the Co-operative Housing Federation of Canada (www.chfc.ca). Or, equally you could search for the university you are planning to attend and then search their site for references to co-op housing. But sometimes it is more exciting and more fruitful to cast a wider net.

> Finding co-operative information on a less well-developed subject, or in a country without as extensive Internet networks as Canada and the U.S., can be challenging.

Recently, I did a Google.ca search for "co-operative housing" and found an amazing site about an equally amazing housing co-operative at the University of California, Berkeley Campus. Seeing evidence of the community that the Berkeley Co-op had created reminded me of the importance of the relationships that we build with our neighbours. I was so struck by the Berkeley example (it is a testament to the quality of their website that they were able to communicate something as ephemeral as a sense of community) that I am now considering attending that University: at least, I am now looking into Housing Co-operatives more seriously, and they comprise a much greater factor in my evaluation of prospective universities.

Other sites that turned up were the Guelph Campus COOP and the Neill-Wycik Co-op Residence. And, through the lists of links on these sites, I found many additional housing co-operatives throughout North America.

Finding co-operative information on a less well-developed subject, or in a country without as extensive Internet networks as Canada and the U.S., can be challenging. An important hint is to find main hub pages in the country, be they government websites, or even travel websites, and to search those sites. Generally, governments and large companies who are in the business of providing information have extensive databases of companies and organizations and their contact information. This is a great way to get a phone number or email address: the first big lead in your search. Other ways include checking out the International Co-operative Association Website at www.ica.coop, and soon, the Co-op Learning Centre, www.learningcentre.coop.

In general, it is important to stop and think about the information which you are seeking before you set out on your Internet journey. Blindly plunging into the Internet portal is a sure-fire way to end up engrossed in something totally unrelated to your current search, or aimlessly flipping through page after page of visually stimulating, but mostly unrelated information.

You must ask yourself: What am I looking for? Where would this information be hosted? How can I best get to that source? These questions will lead you to where you need to go.

Here is an example:

1. *What am I looking for?* A farming co-operative in Africa.

2. *Where Should I begin?* The co-operative probably does not have its own website, but a quick search on Google.ca (type in "Africa and co-operative and farming") will make sure.

3. *Where will this information be hosted?* It is likely that international organisations may have been involved with this co-operative through funding or support. Go to the ICA website (www.ica.coop), and also search the International Labour Organisation (www.ilo.org), and the United Nations (www.un.org). Through these searches you may find a report with the name and country of an African farming cooperative.

4. *How can I best get to the source?* Just in case, always search for the name of the co-operative – you never know, it may come up. If this fails, search the country and you will find either a government website or another large website. Begin searching these websites for the name of the group that you have found, or the words cooperative and/or farming. Most times, after a few tries at each of these stages, you will be able to find a co-operative that fits the parameters of your original goal.

Contacting the co-operative you have found will often lead to important information that can be useful in finding more co-operatives. Again the important thing is to prepare beforehand and ask the right questions. If you were to contact an African farming co-operative you may want to ask them who they work with, if they know of any similar co-operatives, how they got started – did any organizations help them? How can those organizations be reached? And so on.

Finding co-operatives on the Internet can be as easy as asking the right questions, or as hard as spending hours of aimless wandering.

Nicole Ghanie, Kenya
Nicole Ghanie graduated from the Environmental Studies programme at York University and was an intern at the International Development Research Centre in Ottawa in summer 2003. Her honours thesis explored the issue of AIDS in Africa and sustainable development. She completed a York International Student Exchange at the University of Amsterdam in 2001-02 and was one of fifty York students chosen in 2003 by York International to participate in the conference titled "Emerging Global Leaders." She has worked extensively with the Alliance for South Asian AIDS Prevention (ASAAP), a non-governmental organization (NGO) dedicated to outreach and education about healthy sexuality for South Asian communities in Toronto. Currently, she is furthering her work on HIV/AIDS prevention in Kenya.

CO-OPTING HIV/AIDS:
African Youth
Fighting HIV/AIDS
THROUGH CO-OPERATIVES

Nicole Ghanie

HIV/AIDS continues to ravage the social networks and productive capacity of African co-operatives. In the fight against HIV/AIDS, the role of co-operatives, and especially the role of young people in co-operatives, needs to be identified and acted upon.

Youth in African co-operatives are heavily affected by HIV/AIDS, through both its illnesses and its socio-economic impacts. This paper draws upon the experiences of Kenyan youth, primarily involved in fishing and agricultural co-operatives, to explore the current co-operative response to HIV/AIDS in Kenya. It provides critiques of how co-operatives and others are dealing with HIV/AIDS, and it comments on the role of young people in developing effective co-operative strategies to battle HIV/AIDS. It argues that, while co-operatives have the potential to be a vehicle for fighting HIV/AIDS, their weaknesses and strengths need to be considered when planning for relevant and accessible interventions. Youth within co-operatives need to be encouraged to be potential champions for HIV/AIDS mitigation, prevention and care.

HIV/AIDS is a uniquely destructive pandemic in that it particularly disadvantages young people in both their productive and reproductive outputs and capacities. It is the world's fourth most common cause of death after heart disease, strokes and acute lower respiratory infections (Dixon et al, 2001). The other three causes primarily affect people in old age, but AIDS deaths are concentrated among prime-age adults who are at their productive and reproductive peak. Globally, women constitute just under half of the adults with HIV/AIDS, but in sub-Saharan Africa more than 55 percent of infected adults are women, and young women are two to four times more likely to be infected than young men (UNAIDS, 2002). Moreover, youth are bearing the brunt of AIDS' impacts: most people infected are in their twenties and thirties, and they die, on average, around a decade later (UNAIDS, 2004). Recent research predicts that it could get worse (UNAIDS, 2003).

> **Youth are especially vulnerable to the impacts of HIV/AIDS.**

The effects of AIDS in sub-Saharan Africa are worse than anywhere else in the world and the numbers of deaths due to HIV/AIDS are altering population dynamics as well as labour and household structures across sub-Saharan Africa.

JULIA SMITH (LEFT) AND NICOLE GHANIE (R.) AT SONDU WIDOWS' GROUP WORKING WITH CHILDREN AT AN ART AND HIV/AIDS WORKSHOP

Other research has documented how HIV/AIDS has sharply reduced human, social, physical, financial and natural capital within agricultural systems. The Food and Agriculture Organization (FAO) reports that the nine most-affected African countries could lose up to 26 percent of their agricultural labour force within the next two decades (FAO 2002).

Youth are especially vulnerable to the impacts of HIV/AIDS. They are the ones most infected and affected; they are also the ones commonly responsible for helping to mitigate its impacts, such as by contributing extra labour and assets to make up for losses in the household and at the workplace.

Co-operatives and HIV/AIDS

Within co-operatives, HIV/AIDS particularly affects youth participation in both management and production since it increases the number of ill and orphaned dependents, causes the loss of skilled labour, and impairs agricultural and nutritional knowledge networks, all developments that impose continuous and debilitating pressures on young people. In fact, whether it is poor attendance at meetings due to a funeral, or lack of available skilled labour, or widows advocating for their rights to co-operative assets, HIV/AIDS affects many facets of co-operative activity.

Other impacts may also be less direct but even more serious: HIV/AIDS is a terminal illness requiring long-term care that can be a burden on household finances, time and resources, which usually means increased responsibilities for young people. Even more subtly, the stigma associated with HIV/AIDS can prevent openness and honesty about the real reasons behind its transmission, thereby impeding behaviour change, and deepening its impact on families and communities and on the co-operatives that try to serve them.

> Even more subtly, the stigma associated with HIV/AIDS can preventopennessandhonesty about the real reasons behind its transmission, thereby impeding behaviour change, and deepening its impact on families and communities and on the co-operatives that try to serve them.

These pressures add to the problems that many co-operatives in Africa have faced in recent years (such as mismanagement, inadequate marketing expertise, trade liberalisation and unfavourable government policies). They have directly and indirectly forced many co-operatives, like the families of HIV/AIDS sufferers, to sell their assets, thereby risking their future sustainability.

HIV/AIDS' impacts on co-operatives:

- Loss of labour supply and remittance income.
- Reduced attendance at member meetings (often due to attending funerals).
- Declining participation in savings and credit schemes.
- Reduction in land under cultivation.

- Declining yields and crop variety, and increased fallow fields and pests.
- Decline in livestock production and health.
- Increased food insecurity and an increase in short-term coping strategies.
- Youth suffering insurmountable despondency and hopelessness in relation to economic prospects.
- Impaired income generation and diversification (both farm and non-farm).
- Loss of productive land and assets (women often lose access to land).
- Loss of agricultural, technical and nutritional knowledge.
- Decrease in environmental management (e.g., soil conservation).
- Diversion of co-operative resources (such as sale of assets or diverting credit to care for sick and dying).

We can use Kenyan co-operatives as an example of how co-operatives are responding to the pandemic. Because of their membership bases, community influence, and local leaderships, co-operatives have been widely used for prevention education and behaviour change programmes. While this is an effective component of fighting HIV/AIDS, it has its weaknesses when implemented in isolation from other components, such as care and mitigation, and the nature of the livelihood activities of the communities.

Prevention education aimed particularly at young people is a popular tool in the battle against the pandemic for a variety of reasons. First, the donor and development agencies and faith-based organizations popularly advocate it in their efforts to stop the spread of HIV. Second, it requires low intensity planning for integration into other existing activities since AIDS can be easily integrated into programming by setting aside a few days a year for outreach. Training of trainer programs, another popular tool of prevention education, requires little change in programme design, monitoring and evaluation. Finally, it can reach large numbers of people at one time and in one repeatable way. Seminars can be replicated in various areas without much change in information or the way that information is presented.

> [Co-ops] could provide information and leadership on the problems associated with multiple sex partners, drug and alcohol abuse.

How effective, though, are prevention education strategies in fighting HIV/AIDS in co-operatives? Is the level of knowledge gained adequate or is behaviour modified? It is difficult to know the impact of general "AIDS 101" talks on communities already infected with and affected by HIV/AIDS?

The following section debates these issues by first looking at the potential of co-operatives to fight HIV/AIDS, and second at the critiques of the current approaches to mainstreaming HIV/AIDS in co-operatives. In the process, it shows how youth involvement is essential to long-term success.

This approach, though, is only part of what co-operatives – and particularly the young people associated with them – could do. They could help address the socio-economic circumstances that contribute to the spread of the pandemic and cases in point can be found in Kenya. For example, fishing co-operatives around Lake Victoria in Kenya often pay fisherman on a daily basis, thus creating "hot money" that is regularly spent promptly on sexual partners, alcohol, and drugs. They could help counteract this by encouraging strong and reliable savings and credit options for members, thereby reducing the amount of "hot money" available. They could provide information and leadership on the problems associated with multiple sex partners, drug and alcohol abuse. They could show members the impact of such practices on the number of fish caught and sold, and their effects on sustainability and profit. Doing so could encourage members to become active participants in fighting the pandemic while simultaneously helping them improve their livelihood and to develop the co-operative.

> "Sex for fish" is the result of [female fish trader's] poor bargaining power and weak financial organisation.

The co-ops could also encourage programmes to help fish traders, who are usually female. They are in constant interaction with fishermen who are members. Fish traders, caught in fierce competitive situations and with low incomes, not uncommonly resort to having sexual relations with fishermen as they compete for the day's catch. "Sex for fish" is the result of their poor bargaining power and weak financial organisation. Co-operatives could help by providing fish traders with training in savings and credit, good business practices, and improved financial management. They could also help provide economic alternatives for women in situations of domestic violence and provide information on the critical connections between patriarchy, HIV/AIDS and business.

In short, co-operatives, as some in Kenya, Uganda and India, are doing, could more fully integrate HIV/AIDS into their regular training programmes and address more completely the problems stemming from HIV/AIDS on their business activities (see list below). Doing so would allow the co-operatives to help communities address the complexity of issues associated with the pandemic.

Integrating HIV/AIDS concerns into co-operative business practices:

- Incorporate business and HIV/AIDS information into training of trainer programs for co-op committee members and managers.
- Train managers on how to calculate the impacts of HIV/AIDS on business.
- Discuss workplace HIV/AIDS policies to promote institutionalization of HIV/AIDS awareness and support.
- Recognize the impacts of HIV/AIDS on women's income generating activities.

- Understand the impacts of HIV/AIDS on co-operative development activities, such as income diversification strategies.
- Understand the impact of HIV/AIDS on marketing, productivity and labour supply.

Another example can be found in the Nyanza province of Kenya, where the Sondu Widows' Group carries on its work according to principles and activities that are very much like those of a co-op. The province has the highest HIV/AIDS prevalence rate in Kenya, currently at 24.5 percent (Ministry of Health statistics, Kisumu District 2004). While prevention education is still valuable in this context, of greater importance is the kind of support these women need in fostering the orphans of dead relatives and maintaining their small businesses. Women need to secure inheritance rights to the land and to learn how to mitigate the impacts of lost labour on their farms. Their greatest needs are land rights for widows, community vocational training for orphans, and start-up savings and credit organisations with services that respond to households caring for sick members.

> Sondu Widows' Group carries on its work according to principles and activities that are very much like those of a co-op.

Other options and strategies for co-operatives are to:

- Create resilient production systems.
- Participate in savings and credit schemes and other co-op partnerships.
- Share good practices with other co-ops and similar institutions.
- Respond to changing agricultural needs, such as providing lighter and stronger tools for use by women and youth.
- Diversify production to maintain environmental and financial sustainability.
- Create partnerships with training, counselling and awareness services.
- Lobby for extension and co-operative services that are youth and gender friendly.
- Diversify household income.
- Understand and respond to the double burden on young and old women caring for orphans and sick in households.
- Promote urban-rural networking (for example market linkages).
- Mobilize youth and elders to reduce the stigma around HIV/AIDS.
- Increase access for women to technology, credit and supportive networks.
- Promote youth networks and sharing of agricultural and management knowledge.
- Promote youth leadership.

- Advocate against gender-based violence and abuse by youth of drugs and alcohol.
- Increase training for managers on HIV/AIDS sensitization.
- Understand the link between HIV/AIDS and the bottom line (measuring financial impacts, planning for business continuity, business mentoring, writing wills, how to develop a sustainable and effective co-op workplace HIV/AIDS program).
- Help manage STDs amongst youth through information, treatment and increased nutrition, particularly of women and children.
- Increase access to clean and sanitary water.
- Promote youth participation in urban and household agriculture (including small animal husbandry).

Gender and HIV/AIDS

Co-operatives could also help in coping with the fact that young women and girls disproportionately suffer from the impacts of HIV/AIDS. In several Africa countries, infection rates among young women (under 24 years) are two to six times higher than among young men. Many women experience sexual and economic subordination in their personal relationships and at work, and so cannot negotiate safe sex or refuse unsafe sex. The traditional domestic and nurturing

DORIS GIVES SOME SEEDS TO MEMBERS OF THE SONDU WIDOWS' GROUP

roles of women mean that they bear most of the burden of care – this not only adds to their workload but also undermines the vital productive, reproductive and community roles they play. A 2003 UN Population Division study in Tanzania found that women whose husbands were sick spent up to 45 percent less time doing agricultural or income-earning work than before illness struck.

How do we address gender, co-operative business and HIV/AIDS?

- Train young women and girls on income diversification, savings and credit.
- Create spaces and opportunities for young women to participate in meaningful leadership.
- Address sexual exploitation in business practices (e.g., Sex-for-food).
- Diminish cooperative policies that are gender biased or gender blind.
- Ensure inheritance rights (of assets and land) for women and girls.
- Training on personal/household budgets.
- Increase economic empowerment of women and girls.
- Addresses gendered aspects of cooperative organization and activity (i.e. market and credit access).
- Take a no-tolerance stance against gender-based violence.
- Involve young men in gender sensitivity training.
- Support gender integration as good business practice.
- Increase the participation of women and girls in sensitization and TOT seminars.
- Support group initiatives by women outside of formal business employment (i.e. spouses of workers, young women, traders and marketers etc.).
- Gendered HIV/AIDS analysis of business to determine how HIV/AIDS is impacting.
- Determine how changing households and labour forces are affecting gender divisions of labour and household food and economic security.
- Advocate women's sexual rights as human rights supported by the business and it's employees.
- Address alcoholism, drug abuse, domestic violence and other social problems in business community that are increasing vulnerability of women to HIV/AIDS.

The co-operative workplace mirrors, and sometimes exacerbates, gender inequalities and discrimination present in society as a whole. Co-operative programmes for HIV/AIDS need to be sensitive to the gendered impacts of the disease. Co-operatives should be aware of harmful business practices that encourage or condone risk to HIV/AIDS. Co-operatives could exert leadership by showing zero-tolerance for violence and harassment against women at work (e.g., by having procedures for complaints that are simple and accessible). Mainstreaming gender issues in HIV/AIDS programming within organisations can result in more effective responses to the pandemic.

Conclusions

Successful and sustainable HIV/AIDS prevention involves more than strategies for encouraging positive individual behaviour change. While personal behaviour modification is a critical component of a comprehensive HIV/AIDS program, it should not be regarded in isolation. The environment in which behaviour change occurs is crucial in understanding the values, pressures, and rationale behind actions. Activities in the co-operative sector for HIV/AIDS mainstreaming have usually included such activities as sensitisation seminars, training of trainer programs, prevention education, and encouraging VCT and condom use.

A deeper kind of HIV/AIDS mainstreaming would make use of the mass mobilisation networks that co-operatives are built upon. It would effectively utilize the comparative advantage and expert knowledge that already exists in the development programmes associated with co-operatives. It would utilize the mobilisation capacity of co-operatives to situate the struggle against HIV/AIDS within other crosscutting issues common in co-operative development strategies, such as gender, youth and human rights. It would encourage consideration of other marginalized and vulnerable groups, such as widows, orphans and female-headed and child-headed households.

> Many women experience sexual and economic subordination in their personal relationships and at work, and so cannot negotiate safe sex or refuse unsafe sex.

In short, helping to mitigate the environmental causes of vulnerability and susceptibility is ultimately the most promising way for co-operatives to help fight HIV/AIDS. Co-operatives need to think more about the impact of gender, youth, and people living with HIV/AIDS and to understand how special attention and differential treatment for such groups will affect co-operative development. Co-operatives need to understand more fully the diverse and complex ways in which the pandemic is affecting them, including the loss of labour and market opportunities. They need to be sensitive to the double burden of care for women and girls in their communities.

Using an HIV/AIDS-lens requires careful planning, gender sensitivity and community participation at all stages (from design, to implementation, to evaluation) in the development of a comprehensive approach. In combating HIV/AIDS, it is important that co-operatives are inclusive of marginalized and vulnerable peoples, such as young women and girls, and people living with HIV/AIDS. There is a need, which co-operatives could help meet, to develop specific indicators for success with HIV/AIDS mainstreaming. HIV/AIDS indicators should become part of the larger indicators of any development programme in which co-operatives are engaged, so that everyone will understand both the intended and unintended health successes arising from community economic empowerment strategies.

How can we effectively mainstream HIV/AIDS into cooperatives?

- Conduct a baseline study on HIV/AIDS prevalence at co-op project sites prior to project implementation.
- Create success indicators that capture intended and unintended results of general health.
- Design indicators to reflect the unique challenges of both men and women living with and affected by HIV/AIDS.
- Increase relevance and accessibility of information to marginalized groups
- Increase inclusiveness of youth living with HIV/AIDS.
- Determine how specific activities/initiatives are different in a context where HIV/AIDS has changed dynamics of households and labour forces.
- Determine the risk and/or vulnerability of groups benefiting from the project.
- Communicate with the community to determine the need for HIV/AIDS training, level of awareness and social attitudes around sexuality.
- Coordinate with other NGOs that are providing HIV/AIDS information to cooperatives.
- Evaluate the impact on employees (e.g., trained members are dying, funerals interrupt meetings).
- Develop monitoring tools that map the outcome of other partners also working at project sites.
- Evaluate HIV/AIDS mainstreaming as part of overall health, livelihood and ecosystem improvement, as opposed to just infection or prevalence rates.
- Encourage youth to become involved in leadership positions.
- Appoint youth focal persons to monitor HIV/AIDS activities.
- Mobilize youth around fighting discrimination of people living with HIV/AIDS and stigmatization.

In this context, the support and engagement of youth is particularly important. Co-operatives can be effective instruments for mobilizing young people to understand and to work against the immediate and contextual causes of the HIV/AIDS pandemic. They could help significantly in combating the social, legal and economic contexts that contribute markedly to the deepening crisis. Their energy, vitality and knowledge should serve as an important root for co-operative sustainability in the face of the pandemic.

NICOLE AND C.E.E.D.C.O. FACILITATOR ELIZABETH ANGWECH VISITING FARMS CREATED BY FISHERMAN AS AN INCOME DIVERSIFYING STRATEGY

DONNA ST. LOUIS IN FRONT OF A GROUP OF SECONDARY SCHOOL STUDENTS AFTER A YOUTH SAVINGS CLUB PRESENTATION.

Donna St. Louis, Ghana
Donna is a Youth Savings Intern at the Ghana Cooperative Credit Union
Association. Her work is sponsored by the Canadian Cooperative Associa-
tion and the Canadian International Development Agency.

10

YOUTH SAVINGS CLUBS IN GHANA:

Building Brighter Futures for Youth, Increasing Tolerance and Education Towards HIV/AIDS

Donna St. Louis

The Youth Savings Club programme is a capacity building project for the Ghana Co-operative Credit Union Association (CUA). The credit union movement in Ghana is nation-wide with millions of members and billions of cedis in savings. Yet, the majority of the membership is between the ages of 45-60. In order to attract a younger member base, CUA has started 'mini' credit unions or Youth Savings Clubs in senior secondary schools throughout the country.

A recent graduate of O'Reilly Senior Secondary School in Accra, Edmund Agbeve, was a driving force behind the starting up of a Youth Savings Club at his school in 2004.

Edmund's dedication to the programme was tireless, and he was able to recruit over 100 students to join the club and convince them to actively save. Within a short time, O'Reilly Secondary School had over 4 million cedis in savings – the equivalent to $570 Canadian dollars.

Each club is designed after the co-operative credit union model. Participating student members elect a board of directors and decide on the policy and procedures operating under their own by-laws patterned after the Model By Laws of the credit union system in Ghana. They are encouraged to save small amounts collected by an elected Treasurer who gathers savings each day. The students save collectively and open one account with a credit union or bank. Many Clubs have saved enough to invest their money and collect interest. Currently, the clubs have over 100 billion cedis in savings with over 4,000 members.

Edmund's motivation to help youth save is simple. "When you save money, you know you have a bright future…when you save, you have money to do what you want, or need to do," he emphatically states. When asked how students are able to save without being employed, Edmund explained that "we get a little from our parents each day. If we take 2,000 cedis for school, save as little as 200 cedis per day then we can achieve something. By the end of the term we have some money."

A TEACHER, MR. OKRAKU ANSAH, WITH A YOUTH SAVINGS CLUB MEMBER

A STUDENT MAKING A DEPOSIT

The benefits for the students are far reaching. While many develop the habit of saving, they watch their savings accumulate and after three years, some students will save over 1 million cedis. To date, students have been able to use their savings for paying university fees, starting small businesses, and helping their families during emergencies. For example, one member was able to use her savings to help her family purchase a deep freezer, which was used to store pure water sachets to sell as ice. With the profits that her family made from the sales of the pure water, she was able to pay for her entrance fees to Cape Coast University. Another student was able to help her family rebuild after a fire destroyed their home.

The Youth Savings Club project also has an HIV/AIDS component where youth are invited to participate in Peer Education projects. Youth, selected by their peers, are trained to educate their classmates on issues related to sexual health, relationships and HIV/AIDS. The programme effectively uses creative ways to educate the students, including drama, debates, creativity contests and quizzes.

Edmund was selected as a peer educator at his school and helped to provide a HIV/AIDS Peer Education activity for his classmates. The event included a short drama about the consequences of contracting HIV/AIDS and a presentation by a person living with HIV. Because of his participation as a peer educator, Edmund says, "Before, I had the perception that only people with wicked minds would talk about or use condoms. Now, I can talk freely about condom use with my peers or with adults. They are the best way of protecting oneself from STD's."

Edmund's perception of HIV has also changed: "I have more compassion for people living with HIV/AIDS. By chance I met someone with HIV/AIDS, she sat by me and we ate at the same table. I met another woman who is HIV positive and we shook hands. After listening to their stories, I learned that it could happen to me, why should I discriminate?"

Now finished secondary school, Edmund is preparing to study journalism at the Ghana Institute of Journalism. In the meantime, he is busy advocating for youth issues and assisting CUA's Youth Team with training more youth in Peer Education.

In an interview, Edmund recalled his involvement in the Youth Savings Club as follows.

EDMUND AGBEVE

My Story – A Humble Beginning

by Edmund Agbeve, Accra, Ghana

On a hot afternoon in February 2004, when I was the Student Representative Council's president, I was called by the headmistress of my school. On my way to the office I met a lady who was in red attire. I ignored her and briskly in no time I got to the office. I later got to know her as Miss Betty Mensah, who is now known as Mrs. Betty Adu-Asare, the National Coordinator of the Youth Savings Club.

In the office of the headmistress I met two Canadian ladies who introduced themselves as members of the Youth Savings Club team. Their purpose in coming was to tell me and the boy's prefect of the school about the idea of forming a club that would encourage youth to save the little money they have. The idea was a laudable one, so we decided to support it.

We were then tasked to look for a committed and dedicated teacher who would support the YSC. We diligently searched and found Ms. Quansah. She has been the backbone for the club to date in O'Reilly. A week later we were invited to attend the first ever Youth Savings Club Conference in Takoradi. At the conference, we met some other participants from other schools. We shared ideas on how to best educate our peers on HIV AIDS in our schools and communities.

Difficulties

It was very difficult getting some of the students to join the club – especially the final year students who at the time were giving me a lot of problems. Some of the students were very skeptical about the whole concept of introducing a club of that kind in the school. They thought the people were there to dupe them but fortunately we explained to them and some of them understood and agreed to join the club. We gave out over 300 membership forms but only 100 were returned. Even amongst those who returned the forms only a handful saw the need to save money. I had to be very tolerant because the students had the perceptions that I was using their monies for my personal use but I explained to them that I had records of their monies but I don't keep them. Sometimes I had to miss class to make sure things were okay.

Success

Now in its tenth month in O'Reilly, the club is growing in strength. The Youth Savings Club has had some success and we have invested some of our monies. The Club has shares worth over four million cedis in four major companies in Ghana. The companies include: Cocoa Processing Company, producer of the world's number one chocolate. Mechanical Lloyd, distributors of BMW Cars, Range Rovers and Land Rovers. Clydstone, an ICT Company serving the whole of West Africa and Ghana. Breweries Ltd which produces Amstel Malta, Club Beer and more. The Club also saves money with the Credit Union Association (CUA) National Office. In May 2004, the Youth Savings Club in O'Reilly Secondary was the first school in Ghana to have organized an HIV AIDS Peer Education programme following the Youth Conference in Takoradi. The club also contributed articles to the YSC Newsletter and won the "Star School" of the month sponsored by CUA's YSC Team. v

Hopes

I'm hoping the YSC would grow in O'Reilly and other schools across the world. This will go a long way to make the youth an independent being rather than a dependent being.

A YOUTH SAVINGS CLUB MEMBER AT TAKORADI SENIOR SECONDARY SCHOOL

PART TWO:

Youth Developing Co-operatives

In the co-operative world, few things are as important as the ways in which groups perceive and then pursue opportunities for co-operative enterprise. The following case studies illustrate some of the ways in which young people in different parts of the world are engaging in co-operative activities: what has been important to them, how they have taken advantage of opportunities, and what they have accomplished.

The co-operation revealed in what follows takes place on different levels. Some of it emerges out of traditional co-operation as practised in families and communities for generations, if not for ages. Some of it is spontaneous, the result of people coming together to do something to contend with various issues in their communities and societies, an instinctive activity that has always characterized human adaptation – at least as much as the more widely publicized competitive tendencies. Some is structured within formal co-operative organisation as defined by statutes and regulated by governments – the kind of co-operative activity that the organized international co-operative movement particularly appreciates.

All of the cases, though, demonstrate a strong determination to employ the co-operative model to meet important needs, perhaps most commonly, to find employment and empowerment in circumstances where doing so is difficult. They also show the pride youthful members take in what they build, in their roles as pioneers in the places in which they live, and as participants within a global co-operative impulse that can particularly embrace young people.

The Editors

Omar Bhimji, Canada

Omar studied law at UBC and volunteered at the AMS Bike Co-op and Our Community Bikes – a Vancouver based bike cooperative. Omar became the president of the AMS Bike Co-op in 2004. Omar recently graduated and is presently working for Bikes Not Bombs in South Africa.

University of British Columbia
youth TURNING THE WHEELS OF CHANGE!

Omar Bhimji

Erica Mah, one of the mechanics at *Our Community Bikes*, draws in many of the shop's female customers. Unused to seeing women employed in such a trade and drawn in by the shop's focus on education and a do-it-yourself philosophy, these young women often ask a similar question:

"So, how did you get into working with bikes?"

For many of these women, Erica's answer, "The *AMS Bike Co-op* at UBC," doesn't quite compute. At first blush, it is hard to equate a university with a trade. But that's where the *Bike Co-op* comes in. Founded in 1998 by a diverse group of students united in their love of bicycles, the *Co-op*, while formally a club under the auspices of *the Alma Mater Society (AMS)*, the university's student union, is an organisation dedicated to making UBC a better place for cyclists and promoting the social, environmental and health benefits of biking. To this end, the *Co-op* manages a full service repair shop and a community bike fleet, teaches regular workshops on bicycle maintenance and safety, advocates on behalf of the university's cyclists, and holds events to create and celebrate bike culture on campus.

A professionally staffed NGO? Hardly. The *AMS Bike Co-op* was founded, and is run today, by a dedicated group of student volunteers. There is no hiring process or formal training – members who express an interest in contributing to the Co-op are welcomed with open arms, then given a quick tour and free reign to find their own niche. Certain programmes, such as repair workshops, are well established, and require a level of experience by those wishing to contribute. Members wishing to do so attend and assist with clinics, volunteer at the shop and work on their own time, developing the mechanical and teaching skills needed to impart their knowledge to others. Other programmes are defined and driven by individual interests: a plan is hatched, a goal set, and the diverse resources of the *Co-op* and its members are directed towards bringing the idea to life. Art shows, bike festivals, fund-raising calendars, outreach programs, gear libraries – an impressive range of events and projects have emerged from the *Co-op* over the past seven years.

The Co-op provides a nexus that channels student interests and facilitates spontaneous co-operative ventures; its flexible structure and combination of organisational and interpersonal support provide opportunities for even the busiest students. Many of the Co-op's members, now and in the past, juggle full course loads and part-time jobs. This is where the Co-op gives back to its members. Confronted by such challenges as daunting tasks, university bureaucracies, and lack of funds, Co-operatives have demonstrated that through perseverance, improvisation, and a willingness to learn from past mistakes they can make magnificent things happen.

One of the most popular services that the Co-op provides is a fleet of used bikes that are available for use on the UBC campus: the Purple and Yellow Bike Project. Bikes are locked with same-keyed locks, giving all members access to all bikes. If you are a member, whenever you see a bike, you are free to unlock it and ride away. In Autumn 2001, the *Bike Co-op* increased its on

AMS BIKE CO-OP MEMBERS
IN VANCOUVER, CANADA

campus bike system to a total of 230 bicycles. In a university community that has a population of 37,000 undergrad and graduate students, it is clear that cycling is, for many people, the most sensible mode of transportation to, from and around the campus.

There are no shares in the *AMS Bicycle Co-op*. Rather, it charges an annual membership fee that costs twice as much for other members as it does for registered UBC students.

Fees	UBC Student Member	External Member
Full Year (Sept 1 – Aug 31)	$10	$20
2 / 3 Year (Jan 1 – Aug 31)	$7	$15
Summer (May 1 – Aug 31)	$5	$10

Additionally, members who wish to have access to the fleet of Purple and Yellow public bikes are asked to contribute at least three volunteer hours learning how to fix and maintain the bikes.

Community partners like *UBC Trek, Mountain Equipment Co-op* and the *AMS* itself support the Co-op's mission and provide some of the resources needed to carry out an idea. When a member runs into a wall, there's often another member, present or past (something about this organisation makes it tough for people to ever truly "leave"), who can provide help, a new perspective, or timely advice. It's not always pretty, but no one can argue with the results: bike culture and activities flourish on campus, and members emerge from their trials with new skills, experiences and, most importantly, the confidence that only comes with getting something done.

> Co-op alumni who leave to pursue a broad range of interests take with them this sense of agency, along with an appreciation for the benefits of working towards a common goal and getting involved in their community.

Whether it's organizing a trip, teaching a workshop, speaking before a municipal council or finding $250,000 to fund a new community bike centre, members have drawn from their time to work with and direct the *Bike Co-op* in accomplishing incredible things. Co-op alumni who leave to pursue a broad range of interests take with them this sense of agency, along with an appreciation for the benefits of working towards a common goal and getting involved in their community. In this way, the *AMS Bike Co-op* benefits not only its members but also the community at large, by helping to craft responsible, empowered citizens dedicated to making the world a better place – for cyclists and everyone else.

Umsobomvu Youth Fund

Umsobomyu is a Nguni word for "a rising dawn". The Umsobomvu Youth Fund, created in 1998 with a fund of one billion Rand, exists to encourage youth employment, to help young people organize and secure the training to enter into the labour force. Unemployment is a major issue in South Africa, where 7.8 million of the 19 million young people are unemployed – and the numbers of unemployed grow by 400,000 a year. The Fund has helped many young people in South Africa to start new co-operatives. (Excerpt from the Umsobomyu website: http://www.uyf.org.za/)

2

Supported by the Umsobomvu Youth Fund, South Africa

AGANANG
Youth Co-operative

South Africa

Name of the Co-operative: Aganang is a Setswana name meaning "building each other".

Date of Incorporation: The registration documents of the co-operative were submitted in November 2004 for registration with the Registrar of Co-operatives.

Economic Activity

Aganang Youth Co-operative is an agricultural co-operative with the following core business activities;

- Broiler Production
- Vegetable Production
- Pig farming

These seemingly separate activities are located in one area of about 2.5 hectares of land to ensure integration and efficiency in terms of planning and marketing of the co-operative's products.

Organisational Form

The co-operative is organized as a worker co-operative, employing 18 young people (ages ranging from 26 years to 35 years), all of whom were previously unemployed. There are seven females and 11 males in the group, all of them from the village of Makapanstad. Members of the co-operative democratically elect a Board of Directors to manage its activities as well as to monitor policy implementation and compliance with legislation.

Area Served

The co-operative is located in a community adjacent to Hammanskraal Township, Moretele. It is not far from Pretoria, the administrative capital of South Africa.

The co-operative targets Hammanskraal township, the market area of the greater Pretoria area. The co-operative has further targeted the local abattoir, local hospitals and fresh market retailers.

Story of the co-operative

The co-operative was formed in 2001 by local unemployed youth, most of whom held secondary schooling qualifications; some had tertiary level qualifications, such as Diplomas in Agriculture (two people) and Bachelor of Arts in Public Administration (one person).

MEETING IN THE SHADE

The technical skills possessed by this small group were important in the conceptualization of its business activities and the development of its business plan framework.

Aganang Youth Co-operative was founded on the need to create jobs for young people in the community of Makapanstad. From its inception, local community (notably the Tribal Authority), the local municipality, the provincial Department of Agriculture, and other youth organisations in the community have supported the co-operative.

After a series of meetings with the local Tribal Authority, the local Chief allocated the co-operative the 2.5 hectares of land on which it now operates.

After a series of meetings with the local Tribal Authority, the local Chief allocated the co-operative the 2.5 hectares of land on which it now operates.

Local agricultural extension officers, at the request of the chief, together with the youth leadership, took the business framework further and helped produce a business plan for the co-operative. This business plan was then submitted to the Umsobomvu Youth Fund for funding in 2002, and it was approved during the same year.

After the approval of the business plan, the entire co-operative membership was trained in several areas, namely:

- Horticulture
- Broiler Production
- Basic Business Management skills
- Marketing
- Pest Control

These training courses were provided through the collaboration of Umsobomvu Youth Fund and the Department of Labour (Skills Development Unit). Furthermore, the local municipality assisted the co-operative with site clearing by allocating a grader to de–bush the area where the co-operative was developed. The local office of the provincial Department of Agriculture continues to provide on-going support to the co-operative.

Vision/Purpose/Goals

- To establish a secure, affordable food supply chain for the villages of Kudube, Hammanskraal and Greater Pretoria townships through youth co-operatives;
- to employ members in the co-operative; and
- to provide employment opportunities for the broader community.

Mission Statement

To contribute to food security through a vibrant, sustainable and democratic youth co-operative that also creates jobs and fight poverty.

Aganang seeks to grow vegetables organically to ensure sustainable land use, which will result in life-long food security for our communities whilst empowering them to replicate the co-operative model in various economic activities.

Linkages to the community

The co-operative has the following links with the community:

- Makapanstad Tribal Authority
- Local Municipality – Local Economic Development Programme
- Department of Agriculture

Organisational structure

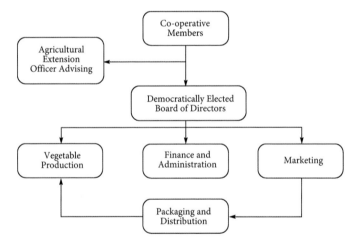

Future plans

The co-operative plans to implement all its plans and effectively increase its market share in the Bakgatla broader community as well as Greater Pretoria. These plans apply to the short and medium-term goals. In the long-term, the co-operative also intends to increase its operations, within the next five years, by acquiring more land so that it can meet the potential increase in the market for fresh vegetables that will be grown.

Lessons Learned

Since the first inception meeting of the co-operative, the following lessons have been learned:

- The importance of working and creating close ties with the broader community.
- The value of involving all members of the co-operative in the decision-making processes.
- That the promotion and development of the co-operative should by all means be driven by their members with the necessary support from government;
- Support from other organisations should not translate into interference.
- The importance of separating roles in the co-operative: for instance, the role of the Board of Directors should be clearly defined from that of management.

The relationship between the co-operative and all the institutions and government departments should be characterized by respect for the co-operative principles and values. In most instances, where educational institutions were trying to support the co-operative, the approach has been similar to those adopted for conventional SMME (Small Medium and Micro Enterprises). This approach has tended to alienate co-operative members from their preferred values and principles and it has tended to divide the co-operative members. There is a need for more educational programmes that faithfully examine co-operative principles and values.

THE BEST LANDSCAPE IN THE SCHOOL WAS
CONTRIBUTED BY THE CO-OPERATIVE.

Dayang Hmsiah bt Mohtar,
Malaysia

Dayang Hamsiah is a teacher by profession, specialising in Living Skills and Commerce for Form 1 and Form 3 students. This mother of six children lives in Enggor, Perak. She has been involved in the school co-operative movement for 16 years. She is currently the Treasurer of the SBS Co-op.

3 SIMPANG BELURU
Secondary School Co-operatives Limited

SBS Co-op

Dayang Hmsiah bt Mohtar

Date of Incorporation: 10 June 1997

Membership: Total number: 858. People: Students, Teaching and Non-Teaching Staff, ages 13 to 50 yrs.

Activity: Consumer, service, rental, and tourism

Organisational Form: Consumer Co-operative

Area Served: School Members

Introduction

Our school co-operative is situated in a village about 30 km from the nearest town in Kuala Kangsar, Perak, Malaysia. The local economic activity is mainly rubber planting. Since one would need to go to the town to get school and house provision and supplies, the co-operative was set up to serve and meet the basic needs of our members. We have 858 members, including 818 students, male and female, 34 teachers, and 6 non-teaching staff. The students are between twelve and seventeen years old.

As the school is focused on providing education for its students, the co-operative focuses on the business activities associated with that activity. The members plan the co-operative's main activities, thereby having many opportunities to develop their entrepreneurial skills. The co-operative's profits are returned back to its members in the form of a dividend payment to the school through community programmes. It is a model that has thrived in almost all secondary schools in Malaysia.

Activities

The SBS Co-op began humbly in a small room in 1997, selling stationery items, sportswear, neckties and nametags to students. Its activity has since grown in number and range. The co-operative's activities today are divided into 3 categories:

A. Economic Activities

1. Convenience Shop – Selling of stationery items, souvenir items, sportswear, food and drinks.

2. Services

   ▫ Launderette service

   ▫ Rental of covered parking space to teachers and staff

   ▫ Copying, binding and laminating service

   ▫ Savings centre

3. ICTs Service – The co-operative offers computer classes and Internet services to its members.

B. Educational Activities

The co-operative participates in events jointly organized by the Ministry of Education and the National Co-operative Organisation of Malaysia (ANGKASA) – the apex body for the co-operative movement in the country. It sends members to the Administrative and Management Course and the School Co-operative Tourism Project.

C. Social Activities

1. Sports and Recreation: The co-operative organizes Petanque tournaments among its members and other co-operatives.

2. Community Service: The co-operative contributes cash and books to deserving students during the school's Prize Giving Day, Teacher-Student's Day and SportsR Day. It also provides donations to needy students.

COMPUTER CLASSES ESPECIALLY FOR CO-OP MEMBERS ARE CONDUCTED IN A CYBER CAFÉ OWNED BY THE CO-OPERATIVE.

Management

The school co-operative by-laws require the Principal of the school to be a member and to be the chairman of the school co-operative board. Other board members include other members of the school staff and students elected by the members at the Annual General Meeting. SBS Co-op is managed by fifteen Board Members (ten students, five teachers) and three Internal Auditors (two students, one teacher). The students play a major role in the decision making process in running the co-operative.

In addition, the Board appoints a committee to oversee the collection of savings from members. Two co-operative members from each class are elected to the committee, and there are a total of 50 co-operative members on the committee to handle the cash deposited by the co-operative members. Other members of the committee ensure that the other services provided by the co-operative are running smoothly. The minimum share for the students in SBS Co-op is RM3.00 while the staff member is RM10.00.

The Success

The SBS Co-op has been successful because of the strong commitment of its Board of Directors and its members. Though the teachers are occupied with teaching and students with schoolwork, it has not been a deterrent for them to contribute to the co-operative and ensure that it operates effectively and successfully. Guidance from

THE CO-OP'S MOST POPULAR SERVICE – THE TELEPHONE.

the apex organisation and the Ministry of Education has played a critical role in our success.

The services offered are customized to the needs of the students. The co-operative charges reasonable fees to its members for such services as the launderette, computer classes, and Internet access. It operates a one-stop centre for students where they can purchase their stationery, postage, and daily supplies.

SBS Co-op has a sound and proven financial track record and therefore enjoys strong support from local wholesalers and suppliers. It has successfully accumulated some assets and has been able to put aside a substantial amount of cash in a fixed deposit account as a result of prudent management of the accounts and administration. The financial record at end of April 2003 showed that the co-operative had managed to record an accumulated profit of RM43,281.94, an increase of fifteen per cent from the amount recorded in previous years. It also showed the co-operative's current assets stood at RM53,529.65 against the current liabilities of RM4,265.80. Analysis on its liquidity showed that its current ratio is 12.5 times. This is a very strong position for the co-operative, allowing it to repay its creditors and to pay its short-term loans.

It is to the SBS Co-op's credit that it has contributed significantly towards school development. For the period of 1999-2002 a total of RM13,049.00 was spent and this includes students' rest area, play area for Petanque, Bougainvillaea Rest Area, Reflexology Signboards, School Platforms one and two, and curtains for the prayer room.

In recognition of their sound management, record of activities organized and involvement of members, SBS Co-op has received the following awards:

- State Co-operative Quality Award conferred by The Department of Co-operative Development of Malaysia.
- Best School Co-operative Award (Daily-School Category) conferred by ANGKASA.
- Winner of the Co-operative Quiz Competition at the State Level conferred by ANGKASA.

Based on the experience of the SBS Co-op and other school co-operatives in Malaysia, we believe that the success of such organisations is dependent upon the following characteristics.

- Strong commitment and guidance from the school principals and teachers in establishing the school co-operative and turning it into a successful co-operative.
- Strong involvement by students and teachers in the co-operative's activities.
- Careful management of the business of the co-operative.
- Ability to meet the needs of its community.
- Ability to contribute positively to the development of the school.
- Structured guidance provided by the apex organisation (in our case ANGKASA) and the government's effort towards the development of the school co-operative movement.

MARANG CAKE, BREAD & CATERING CO – OP

Working together for economic participation & job creation

Supported by the Umsobomvu Youth Fund (page 82), South Africa. The Fund has helped many young people in South Africa to start new co-operatives.

4

MARANG

Cake, Bread, & Catering

Co-operative

South Africa

Name of the Co-operative: Marang Cake, Bread and Catering Co-operative. *Marang* is a Setswana word meaning the *"dawn of the new day"*.

Date of Incorporation: 14th July 2001.

Economic Activity: The co–operative is engaged in cake and bread making as well as catering services. It operates in both the manufacturing and services sectors of the economy.

Organisational Form: The co-operative is organized as a worker co-operative. All its members are full-time employees and owners of the co-operative.

Area Served: The co-operative operates within the geographic area surrounding the Mafikeng District Municipality in the North West province of South Africa. It also exports its products to Botswana, the neighbouring state.

Story of the Co - operative

The initial conception was to create a business entity to produce bread and cakes as well as providing catering services to the community developed during the festive season of 2000. The idea came about as a result of four young unemployed people, highly skilled in baking, realising that there was a market in the community for quality baked goods. This realisation came about after they had baked for, and catered to, a local wedding ceremony.

These four young men then decided to pursue the business idea by consulting with their first client (the wedding groom) to discuss the feasibility of their business idea. This client, who possessed a diploma in Human Resources Development in Business Management, decided to join the group, together with his wife, who was also unemployed at the time.

After its first meeting, the group consulted government officials in the office of the Premier of North West Province for advice and assistance with the formulation of the business plan. A number of meetings and consultations followed, after which the group agreed to form a youth worker co-operative with the support of the Department of Agriculture, whose mandate was to promote and support co-operative development in the country. The group had by now grown to seven members and had started a process of recruiting an additional seven young people.

On May 14th 2000, the group held the formal co-operative founding meeting. The minutes and resolutions from that meeting were then sent to the Department of Agriculture for filing, along with further requests for help in training of the newly elected board of directors. The board of directors, composed of five youth leaders, then went through a one-week course of leadership and basic management skills offered by the Department.

Vision / Purpose / Goals

The vision of the co-operative is to provide good quality baked goods for the community through initiatives that create jobs in the community and fight poverty.

Mission Statement

The mission statement of Marang is: to bake and distribute bread products through cost effective methods that will ensure maximum job creation through co-operative enterprise.

The co-operative model was chosen because of its emphasis on equality, equity, and solidarity, and – above all – its commitment to democratic values and principles. It also fits with the needs and aspirations of the members as it empowered them to understand democratic values whilst at the same time insuring economic empowerment. These values have been shared with the broader community.

Starting the Co-operative

As indicated above, four pioneers combined their business concept with their existing baking skills to start the co-operative. Other support has been as follows:

	Organisation	Type of Support
1.	Premier's Office	Initial workshops and linkages
2.	University of North West	Training on Basic Business Management Skills
3.	Department of Agriculture	Training of Board Members
4.	Department of Economic Development per cent Planning	Initial Funding and Capitalisation
5.	NCASA	Training on the co-operative concept
6.	Umsobomvu Youth Fund	Capitalisation of the co-operative and skills development; mentoring support through NCASA; training through the Department of Labour
7.	PRASCO (Progressive Association of Co-operatives)	Continuous training on co-operative concept[s] and linkages.
8.	Entrepreneurial Support Centre (ESC)	Location and security of an operational place for the co-operative; drafting of the business plan

Member contributions also helped fund the first production circle.

Organisational Structure

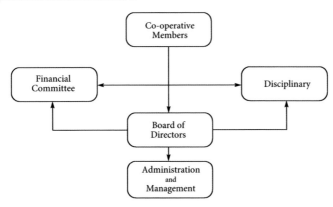

Members elect the board of directors, and it is accountable to them. In addition to the members and the board of directors, two committees have been established. The Financial Committee provides an oversight on financial practices and the Disciplinary Committee monitors adherence to the Co-operative Statute and Code of Conduct.

The general administration and management of production is administered by co-operative worker members.

Initially, co-operative members were not able to draw a salary and worked for the co-operative on a voluntary basis as they wanted the business to grow to a level where it would generate income in a sustainable way. The expectation of members was that once the co–operative had grown to the desired level, they would begin to reap the benefits.

Links to Community

The co-operative has currently provided substantial benefits to local communities by supplying small shops with affordable bread; it has provided 14 young people with some means of a livelihood, and it has assisted in demonstrating the value of the co-operative model to other young people in the community. Today, Marang is assisting in the development of 14 youth co-operatives in the Mafikeng area.

Future plans

In the short term, the co-operative would like to purchase some additional equipment for the bakery and a vehicle to ensure that it is able to produce in greater quantity for sale on the premises or for delivery within a wider market area.

Lessons learned

The co-operative members have learned during the process of establishing their co-operative that there is a need for a collaborative and integrated approach to co-operative development by all stakeholders, such as government departments, municipalities, local educational institutions and civil society organisations. In addition, they have learned the value of co-operation among co-operatives, as they have been able to assist other co-operatives starting up to become established by developing the necessary skills to ensure effective management.

ALL CO-OP MEMBERS ARE FULL-TIME EMPLOYEES AND OWNERS OF THE CO-OPERATIVE

5

STUDENT RUN BUSINESSES
for the University Community

United States of America

The center, located on the campus of the University of Massachusetts in Amherst, Massachusetts in the United States, is committed to helping young people start businesses, especially co-operatives. The co-operatives the Center has helped form provide co-curricular training and education in co-operative management, life skills and business skills in a supportive and diverse setting. They contribute products and services to the University of Massachusett's community and paid employment to undergraduate students. People's Market, Earthfoods, Campus Design and Copy, The Bike Co-op and Tix Unlimited are all located in the Student Union.

People's Market is a natural foods market providing the University community with gourmet coffee, herbal tea, bagels, an assortment of cheeses, fresh fruit and healthy snacks. People's Market supports local and socially conscious vendors.

ONE OF THE CENTER'S SOCIAL EVENTS

Earthfoods is a vegetarian/vegan cafeteria-style restaurant that serves lunch Monday through Friday. All food is prepared fresh daily and a variety of menu items include salad, soup, vegetable, entrée, dessert and beverage.

Campus Design and Copy features photocopying, both color and black and white, graphic design, posters, flyers, resumes and academic packets.

The UMASS Bike Co-op is a full service bicycle repair shop staffed by experienced mechanics and cycle enthusiasts. It offers quality bicycle accessories at competitive prices. Open seasonally.

Tix Unlimited is a student run business that handles ticket sales for all events held on campus by registered student organisations. This group is funded by the Student Government Association and has been mandated by the State to assure that a neutral party will oversee ticket sales and money deposits. Tix also manages the vending operations in the Campus Center.

Three snackbars are located in residence halls. Greenough Sub Shop's menu includes a variety of subs, wraps, hamburgers, bagels, ice cream and a full line of beverages. They also provide catering for on-campus events such as conferences, meetings and parties. Located in Greenough Residence Hall, Greenough is open Sun-Thurs. 5:00 to11:30 PM.

Founded in 1971, Sylvan Snack Bar is the oldest student-managed snack bar on campus. Located in McNamara Residence Hall, Sylvan is open 6 p.m. to 1 a.m. from Sunday through Thursday. It offers great food at competitive prices and also delivers.

> In all of these operations students gain some needed income and learn how to operate a business, notably through co-operative enterprise.

Located in Field Residence Hall, Sweets N'More Snack Bar's menu ranges from brownies, ice cream, and milkshakes to bagels and grilled cheese sandwiches.

In all of these operations students gain some needed income and learn how to operate a business, notably through co-operative enterprise.

ACTIVITIES ON BUS APPRECIATION DAY

CO-OP RUN UNIVERSITY BOOKSTORE IN JAPAN

Roderick C. Bugador, Japan
Roderick Bugador, an international student from the Philippines, is currently a Ph.D. student in the Graduate School of Economics of Kyoto University in Japan. He is a member of the National Foreign Student Network Committee on Co-operatives and the Kyoto University Co-operative.

6

UNIVERSITY CO-OPERATIVES IN JAPAN

Building bridges for the future of their members and the co-operative movement

Roderick C. Bugador

Introduction

Large and successful consumer co-operatives have existed in Japan for many years, and Japanese citizens are known for their positive attitudes towards co-operation. Recently, however, there has been apprehension that the co-operative values system is vanishing. Japanese society is changing rapidly because of globalisation and liberalisation. The majority of active co-operative members used to be housewives, but many housewives are now working and do not have the time to participate in co-ops that they once did. Younger members prefer greater participation in other voluntary groups based on common causes like ecology, welfare, and leisure, rather than the broad, traditional co-operative commitments. Hence, co-operative leaders are becoming increasingly concerned with how to increase member participation.

In addition, recent consumer studies suggest that Japanese youth are now individualistic, rather than collectivistic: for example, they often prefer to meet their socio-economic needs through individual undertakings rather than relying on groups. This may be attributed to incentives, like customized goods and services that are easily accessible, especially through the Internet. Also, a more benevolent government provides public services, and so the need to join any socio-economic enhancement organisations like co-operatives is not apparently as great as it once was. This may be why only a few legitimate youth co-ops can be found in Japan. The drawbacks of this situation for the enhancement of the nation's civil society and for the co-operative movement is alarming, and raises questions about who will form the new generation of co-operators.

> "Organized by both professors and the students, [the co-ops] were formed to help young people in particular to meet a wide range of economic, social, cultural and psychological needs."

However, there is an institution that is continuously addressing this challenge and that particularly emphasizes how young people can meet their economic and social needs through co-operatives: it is the Japanese University Co-operative (*Daigaku Seikyo* in Japanese). These co-operatives existed in Japan even in the pre-Second World War period. Organized by both professors and the students, they were formed to help young people in particular to meet a wide range of

A CO-OP RUN TRAVEL AGENCY

economic, social, cultural and psychological needs. However, along with other types of co-ops, they were shut down by the militaristic government during the Second World War, only to reappear after the war was over.

Today, there are 225 strong university (public, private and inter-college) co-op societies in Japan. They are connected through a network, which represents 1.4 million members, including Japanese and international students (undergraduate and postgraduate). Students make-up 89 per cent of the membership and teaching and non-teaching staff 11 per cent. These co-ops employ nearly 2,000 people and in 2003 had close to $2 billion in turnover. With the help of the Federation of University Co-operatives Association of Japan (NFUCA), the apex organisation, they are organized and supported to promote the co-operative movement and unity among members as they improve the on-campus and off-campus welfare of their members. Members from various classes co-operate with one another, thereby creating the spirit of inclusion, independence, and collaboration.

> Each co-op on a campus is immersed in an atmosphere of learning and encourages the exchanging of experiences as well as helping to promote the building of more positive communities.

Each co-op on a campus is immersed in an atmosphere of learning and encourages the exchanging of experiences as well as helping to promote the building of more positive communities. The co-ops strive to maintain such a unique environment as they work towards the vision of contributing to international student exchanges, peace activities and personal commitment; even as they help members realize their wishes and dreams.

Responding to the socio-economic needs of youth members

The university is not only the place for education and research advancement for students: it also serves as a training ground to help them learn how to undertake their potential future responsibilities as well. Along this vital path, students need guidance and support in every aspect of their life. In their daily living they are far from their families and they often have difficulty in accessing quality goods and services at reasonable prices.

The Japanese university co-ops exist primarily to help students meet these social and economic needs. Their businesses and activities have always been geared to reflect the needs of their members, especially the students.

The Japanese co-ops have several stores with a variety of goods and services, meeting practically all necessities. They sell furniture, appliances and consumer goods. They operate cafeterias that are open from morning until evening. They run bookstores and electronic shops that offer affordable devices and peripherals (in any form and brand) like software, printers, digital cameras, laptops – and much more, depending upon member needs. Such stores accept staggered payments and online purchases.

University co-ops also serve as an entrusted agent, guarantor and consultant when students are looking for better places to live, applying for credit cards, purchasing discounted tickets when traveling inside and outside Japan, attending driving and review schools, and most notably, when they are looking for jobs. All these services may be available in a single university.

> The Japanese co-ops have several stores with a variety of goods and services, meeting practically all necessities.

University co-ops organize various committees for student members, one of which is the committee of student representatives (primary and nationwide). These students are the officers in the general executive body of the co-op. They are expected to uphold and endorse the needs and wants of the rest of the student members. They are also given the highest number of seats in the decision-making process of that co-operative, thereby demonstrating how democratically controlled organisations work.

As for international students, adjustment with the Japanese culture, food, people and especially the language can be tough and may take months or even years; in response to this, co-ops have established the National Foreign Student Network committee. The goal of this committee is to help international students resolve problems that they encounter during their stay in Japan. It also promotes exchanges between Japanese and their fellow international students and with the community by providing offices for consultations and for sponsoring activities like camping, hiking, seasonal parties and field trips. The co-ops also work towards a more humane and environmentally friendly society, achieved through massive recycling campaigns, the supplying of

A CO-OP RUN COMPUTER STORE

ecological products, and participation in local and international peace and environmental movements.

Conclusions

Many people might agree with the saying that youth are the hope of the future. However, in what way and how it will be done is yet uncertain: that is, ideological movements like youth co-operatives can sprout everywhere in any mode, but without dependable structures and resources, this ideology too readily becomes a myth. This is a challenge for everybody; a challenge that the university co-ops in Japan are trying to conquer by serving as institutions that nurture and support the potential of the youth in a crucial period of their lives. These co-ops remarkably enhance students' lives in every aspect, an immense foundation to build upon when they return to their respective communities and journey towards higher horizons. The students who experience the co-op's impartial offerings are developing a deep sense of pride and honour as they are listened to and given importance. From this basis, it is not hard to believe that the youth may shape a desirable future for the Japanese co-operative movement. If they are given enough chances, faith, trust and guidance, they will eventually restore such values to the co-operative movement and to society as a whole.

> The students who experience the co-op's impartial offerings are developing a deep sense of pride and honour as they are listened to and given importance.

STUDENT CONSULTING SERVICES OFFERED BY A CO-OP

THE MBONAMBI CO-OP PRODUCES BRICKS AND BLOCKS

THE BRICKS AND BLOCKS ARE THEN SOLD TO
THE PUBLIC AND TO GOVERNMENT DEPARTMENTS

Supported by the Umsobomvu Youth Fund (page 82), South Africa. The Fund has helped many young people in South Africa to start new co-operatives.

7

MBONAMBI
Youth Co-operative

South Africa

Date of Incorporation: This co-operative, located in the Zulu Kingdom of South Africa, is still engaged in the registration process. All the necessary documentation has been filed with the Registrar of Co-operatives. The group anticipates being registered in early 2005.

Economic Activity: The co-operative produces bricks and blocks that are sold directly to the public and to government departments.

Organisational Form: The co-operative is organised as a worker co-operative, with all its members working in the co-operative on a full time basis.

Served Area: The co-operative is currently serving communities around Magabheni Township, as well as Durban Metro Council, including Umnini.

Story of the Co-operative

The co-operative was established in 2002 as a group of youth realised that there was a demand for locally produced bricks and blocks, particularly in the Umnini area, which is located along the Durban South Cost. The demand arose as a result of the government's Reconstruction and Development Programme (RDP), which was developed to provide housing in the area. In line with the RDP policy, the Durban Metro sought local suppliers for the construction project. A series of meetings was held with the local chief in a bid to strengthen the position of the co-operative in the tendering processes. The chief, Inkosi Luthuli, supported the co-operative, which was finally awarded the contract to supply blocks and bricks for construction of RDP homes and outside toilets.

Vision/Purpose/Goal of the co-operative

Self–employed youth contributing to community development in a sustainable manner.

Mission Statement

Supplying local contractors with quality and affordable bricks and blocks in a manner that seeks to achieve the following core objectives of the co-operative:

- Job creation and poverty eradication;
- Local empowerment of young people;
- Entrenchment of democratic principles and tolerance in the broader community; and
- Instilling in young people the spirit of productivity and social responsibility.

Organisational structure

The co-operative elects a board of directors, which supervises the daily activities of the co-operative.

The elected board measures the co-operative's success by referring to its commitment to a three-pronged strategy aimed at addressing the economic, social and cultural aspirations of its members. The three strategic measuring tools are:

- Member participation in the decision-making processes within the co-operative, thereby influencing members to make humane decisions outside the co-operative within their communities;
- At the economic level, the co-operative started with one contract to supply bricks and blocks to the Durban Metro. Currently, the co-operative is supplying other building contractors with blocks of high quality. The number of contracts the co-operative is able to secure is used as a success indicator. Briefly, this indicator measures the economic performance of the co-operative; and
- Another success indicator in the co-operative is the members' interaction within it, including the sharing of skills, information and caring for others.

Starting the Co-operative

The enterprise started from the vision of a single entrepreneur who saw the need to collaborate with other youth in a business entity that was later converted into a co-operative.

When the co-operative began, it had very limited resources. To remedy this, the group applied for a loan from the Umsobomvu Youth Fund, which approved a start-up capitalisation loan of R491,131.00. The money has been used to procure equipment, raw materials, and infrastructure.

Since the start of operations, the co–operative has made an income of R90,200.00 as follows.

- ◻ Membership fees   - R1000.00
- ◻ Sales of blocks   - R89,200.00

Additional resources available in the community, such as land, water and electricity supply, were made available to the co-operative by the local municipality.

Links to Community/Network/Outreach

The co-operative supplies quality resources for housing projects in the community and also participates in local civic organisations.

ALL MEMBERS WORK IN THE CO-OPERATIVE ON A FULL TIME BASIS

In addition, the co-operative participates in the Integrated Development Programme (IDP) in the local community. Through this programme, the co-operative is able to benefit from development programmes in the local community.

Future Plans

The immediate plans of the co-operative are to speed up the process of registration.

The short-term goals of the co-operative are:

- Consolidation of markets in the entire district;
- Member education and training;
- Product diversification and quality improvement; and
- Purchasing of effective and efficient machinery.

Limited financial resources hamper achievement of these goals. However, with support from the Umsobomvu Youth Fund, the local government, and the community – as well as the income generated by the sales in the co-operative – these challenges are being met. The co-operative is well on its way to becoming sustainable.

Lessons Learned

The co-operative has learned some key lessons:

- It was important to develop a well-researched feasibility study to ensure that, when the co-operative started, there was an already identified market for its products;
- The need to identify and assist co-operatives to access government procurement contracts;
- Assistance to co-operatives is needed to ensure good quality products;
- Good funding sources encourages commitment from the co-operators;
- The loan provided by the UYF ensured that the co-operative operated with the sole objective of achieving economic sustainability and financial prudence;
- Co-operatives capitalised by grant funds can succeed.

Jürgen Schwettmann,
Geneva

Jürgen Schwettmann is the chief of the
co-operative branch of the International
Labour Organisation in Geneva.

8

Youth Co-operatives
IN SERBIA

Youth co-operatives have existed in Serbia (and several other former Yugoslav republics) since 1938. Their main purpose is to familiarize young, unemployed people with the world of work by finding them short-term job opportunities. Today, there are some 300 such co-operatives with 200,000 members in Serbia and Montenegro. Youth co-operatives exist in most urban locations of Serbia that have more than 1000 inhabitants. They have formed a national co-operative union with an office in Belgrade The youth co-operatives are fully self-financed and receive no subsidies from the state. They enjoy excellent working relations with both trade unions and employers' organizations.

How does it work?

Young people in the age bracket from fifteen to thirty years can register with the nearest youth co-operative and they will be issued membership cards. Each new member is expected to contribute the equivalent of 3 € to the co-operative's share capital, but this amount is paid only after the youth has found a job through the co-operative. The co-operative then matches the new member's profile with the requirements of different private and public employers who have offered job opportunities. When a suitable opening is found, the young person can work in the respective company for a maximum period of four months. Thereafter, the employer may decide to hire the youth for a longer period of time; if that does not occur, the co-operative will try to find another short-term job opportunity.

> Each new member is expected to contribute the equivalent of 3 € to the co-operative's share capital, but this amount is paid only after the youth has found a job through the co-operative.

While working for an employer, young people are paid and are covered by the social insurance plan. The co-operative accepts youths with any background, from those without any formal education to university graduates. Jobs are offered in a wide range of public and private occupations, such as banks, hospitals, translation services, construction companies etc.[1] About 20% to 30% of those who find a short-term job through the co-operative system are successful in finding permanent employment.

Co-operative aspects

The degree of membership turnover is obviously very high in this type of co-operative. This notwithstanding, youth co-operatives are governed by the general co-operative law of Serbia (adopted in 1996 and currently under revision), and they apply the basic co-operative principles[2] ("one member – one vote"). Each co-operative organizes at least one general assembly (called "the Big Parliament") per year, which elects the board of directors ("Small Parliament"), the president of the co-operatives, and a delegate to the General Assembly of the national union. The management and administration of the co-operative is financed by a 10% deduction from member salaries.[3] The co-operative is in fact doing the entire payroll work for the employers, who transfer the gross salary amount for all employed youth to the co-operative, which then makes various deductions for taxes and social security before paying the individual members.

> The co-operative is in fact doing the entire payroll work for the employers, who transfer the gross salary amount for all employed youth to the co-operative, which then makes various deductions for taxes and social security before paying the individual members.

The national union of youth co-operatives organizes different events for young people throughout Serbia, facilitates co-operation between co-operatives (thus improving the functioning of the labour market), and organizes exchange visits between young co-operators from Serbia and those from our countries.

---

1   At the time of our mission, some 300 youths were employed by the city council of Belgrade to remove snow and ice from the pavements of the city.
2   The back of the membership card lists the co-operative principles, as well as the rights and obligations of members.
3   An eventual surplus at the end of the financial years is being paid into a solidarity fund that helps youth in difficulties.

Impact

Thanks to the Serbian youth co-operatives, every year some 200,000 young people are gaining their first exposure to the world of work and thus improving their employability. Out of those, some 50,000 youth are being hired on a permanent basis. Even those who are not employed permanently do receive a salary during the short-term assignments, and are covered by social protection schemes. The system also familiarizes young people with the co-operative concept, and many of them do form their own co-operatives afterwards.

> *The system also familiarizes young people with the co-operative concept, and many of them do form their own co-operatives afterwards.*

The youth co-operative model encourages youth participation and ownership in a domain, (i.e., job exchange), which otherwise is often driven by profit motives alone. As the president of the national union formulated it: "Co-operatives have a soul".

MEMBERSHIP CARD FOR SERBIAN YOUTH CO-OP

MEMBERS OF THE MOGOTO CO-OPERATIVE

9

MOGOTO

Youth Co-operative

South Africa

Date of Incorporation: The co–operative submitted its registration documents in September 2004.

Membership: There are 3 female and 12 male members in the co-operative, ranging in age from 21 to 34 years.

Economic Activity: Mogoto Youth Co-operative is an agricultural pre-co-operative involved in broiler production and marketing.

Organisational Form: Mogoto is a worker / producer pre-co-operative.

Story of the co-operative

Mogoto is a rural area around Zebediela in the Limpopo province, where a large number of young people remain unemployed. As a result of this challenge, some young people with a vision of creating jobs for themselves worked with others to start a co-operative in 2001. This need was coupled with the desire to serve the community of Mogoto, as well as greater Zebediela, with quality poultry products at affordable prices.

Three young men who had worked in the poultry industry initiated the project and later recruited others who shared the same vision. As the group grew in size, the members resolved to form a co-operative. With the assistance of the local chief, they held a series of meetings in order to formalize the organisation's co-operative structure. The Limpopo Youth Commission also assisted the group by organising study tours to local poultry production plants and abattoirs. This exposure made the group more determined to start their project.

Vision/Purpose/Goals

The vision of the co-operative is to create decent employment and sustainable livelihoods for youth in the community through collectively owned enterprises.

Mission Statement

The mission statement of the pre-co-operative is to provide poultry products to Mogoto and the greater Zebediala at affordable prices whilst creating jobs, fighting poverty and entrenching democratic values and principles in the community.

Starting the Co-operative

As indicated above, three young men with experience in the poultry industry started the project, which they later decided to turn into a co-operative. Most of the young people in this pre-co-operative have secondary educational level qualifications. When the group started out there were no resources available and members used their own money to run the activities necessary to organise the co-operative. During the initial phases, though, the group applied for support from the Umsobomvu Youth Fund (UYF). It approved a loan of R386,800.00 for start–up capital.

Further resources made available to the co-operative included land provided by the local tribal authority. Extension officers from the local Department of Agriculture have also provided assistance, particularly by helping the co-operative develop a business plan.

Like any other new business venture, the co-operative experienced many obstacles during its initial phases, but these were minimised thanks to the funding from UYF. The level of commitment of the co-operative members has never been a problem. The co-operative model further ensured that, whilst the young people participate in the business activity, they are also able to enjoy continuous skills development, learning from each other, and motivating other young people in the community.

In order to measure the success of the pre-co-operative, four success indicators will be used, namely:

- Income generated in the co-operative
- The level of skills improvement
- Replication of the co-operative model by other young people in the community
- Entrenched democratic values by members, not only in the co-operative but also throughout the entire community.

Organisational Structure

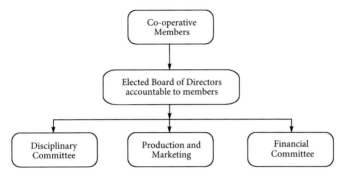

This leadership structure adopted in the co-operative founding meeting has not been changed. The board positions are:

- Chairperson
- Deputy Chairperson
- Secretary
- Deputy Secretary
- Treasurer

The role of this Board is to implement decisions taken at the Annual General Meeting and develop necessary policies for the co-operative to be ratified by members. The Board also manages the co-operative on behalf of members by being responsible for key sections of the co-operative such as production, marketing and administration.

Links to the Community

The co–operative is a community based business entity and therefore links with the community are entrenched in its activities. It consults and reaches agreement with the community in regard to its operations. This process of consultation and concurrence has led to the co–operative being given land by the local chief, who is currently acting as a patron for the co-operative.

Future plans

Currently, the pre-cooperative is intending to start full production beginning in the Spring of 2005 with 3000 broilers increasing to 5000 per cycle. Expansion plans include venturing into vegetable production and into the establishment of an abattoir over the next five years.

Lessons Learned

In most instances it is difficult to organise youth co-operatives, however, with Mogoto the lesson is that young people like doing things for themselves. What needs to be done by all stakeholders is to support the initiatives without dictating and interfering.

MEMBERS EXAMINE A NEW BUILDING

The co–operative has never experienced membership dropout or lack of commitment. This derives from the fact that all members of the co-operative were screened before being accepted. Though the screening process might appear to contradict the values and principles of co-operatives, it has meant that we have committed and loyal members.

10

Supported by the Umsobomvu Youth Fund (page 82), South Africa
The Fund has helped many young people in South Africa to start
new co-operatives.

SBIZUNDLOMBANE
Youth Co-operative

South Africa

Date of Incorporation: The co-operative is in the process of being registered. All the necessary documentation has been submitted to the office of the Registrar of Co-operatives and it is anticipated that it will be formally registered in early 2005.

Membership of the Co-operative: The co-operative has 10 female and 5 male members, ranging in age from 23 to 34 years.

Economic Activity: The core business of the co-operative is broiler production, vegetable production and flower cutting.

Organisational Form: The group is organized into a worker/producer co-operative in the agricultural sector.

Areas Served: The co-operative is located in Durban and is serving the whole area of Durban as well as surrounding townships and villages.

Story of the Co-operative

The group started out as a non-governmental organisation (NGO) in order to facilitate job creation for young people around Durban, Umlazi, and its surrounding areas. It later converted to a co-operative. The group who initiated the development of the co-operative had a variety of skills, which assisted them in getting support from the Durban Metro Council, as well as from other stakeholders in the community. This also encouraged the group to encourage other youth to join the organisation, which is now called Sibizundlombane. Members of the co-operative have achieved the following educational levels:

- Diploma in Agriculture;
- Broiler Production Experience;
- Electrical Engineering; and
- Diploma in Marketing.

We began with a series of meetings to discuss the best business model for what we wanted to do. We chose the co-operative model because it best met the youth's aspirations. After these discussions, we organized a number of workshops to discuss and learn more about the co-operative concept. At the founding meeting, the co-operative statute was adopted, the first Board of Directors was elected, and memberships were confirmed. We then submitted our registration document to the Registrar of Co-operatives.

The co-operative is located in Durban, one of the major harbours of South Africa, which therefore provides a market opportunity for the co-operative. The location also has the potential to expose the co-operative to international markets in the long term.

SBIZUNDLOMBANE FACILITIES UNDER CONSTRUCTION

Vision/Purpose/Goals

To contribute meaningfully to poverty reduction and job creation whilst supporting the formation of other youth enterprises in Durban, Umlazi and surrounding areas.

Mission Statement

The primary purpose of the co-operative is to eradicate poverty and to reverse the trend of youth unemployment through creating self-employment opportunities. The co-operative will achieve its vision through the production of broilers, eggs and vegetables.

The co-operative has sought to utilize the rich skills base of young people in the area in order to reverse the unemployment situation around Umlazi.

The benefits of organizing as a co-operative have been that we have been able to create a business for youth that is receiving adequate support, and to produce high quality products through harnessing the skills possessed by the young people.

The co-operative intends to measure its success in the following manner:

- Providing high quality standards of production;
- Securing markets with government institutions, such as hospitals and prisons;
- Securing dependable markets in the private sector;
- Training highly skilled co-operative members able to produce in an effective and efficient manner; and
- Replicating the co-operative model in the Umlazi community and surrounding areas.

Starting the Co-operative

As indicated above, the group was initially organized as a Non Government Organisation by four young people skilled in agriculture. The co-operative emerged when we decided to convert the existing NGO into a co-operative.

From the beginning, the group was supported by Durban Metro Council in terms of funding and land allocation. The Umsobomvu Youth Fund assisted the co-operative to procure equipment and to build poultry production units. The support from UYF included a loan as well as skills development and mentorship support for a period of one year.

Organisational Structure

The members own a broiler production unit and a marketing agency through their co-operative. They democratically elect their Board of Directors. The board develops the co-operative's policies and procedures. The co-operative has not yet appointed a management unit to manage the day-to-day affairs of the co-operative, which are currently carried out by members of the board.

At the founding meeting, it was agreed that each member would be required to hold a share valued at R300.00, to be deducted from the member's earnings until the full amount is recovered.

Future plans

In the long term, the co-operative intends to expand its activities to include upholstery services and waste recycling.

Lessons Learned

The following lessons have been learned by the co-operative:

- The importance of an integrated approach to co-operative support and development;
- The value of a sound feasibility study and well-researched business plan;
- The importance of skills development as a basis of the co-operative's success and viability; and
- The importance of electing the correct leadership in the co-operative, people who understand the co-operative concept and who allow members to contribute to the organisation's decision-making processes.

Amita Dharmadhikary-Yadwadkar, India

Ms. Amita Dharmadhikary-Yadwadkar holds a doctorate in Economics from the Gokhale Institute of Politics and Economics, Pune, India. She specializes in Applied Macroeconomics and Development Economics. She has observed and studied co-operatives, specifically, women self-help groups in India, in rural development and poverty alleviation efforts. She was involved in an evaluation study of the project, Development of Women and Children in Rural Areas undertaken by National Institute of Bank Management, Pune. She has also written about the Maharashtra Rural Credit Project. She is currently a visiting faculty member at the University of Pune and Centre for Development Studies and Activities, Pune.

11

REDISCOVERING CO-OPERATIVES
for Employment and Income Generation

A Case Study of the Utkarsh Purush Bachat Gat in Kedgaon

Amita Dharmadhikary-Yadwadkar

This is an account of how 10 enterprising young men residing in a small village named Kedgaon in the Pune district of India have rediscovered the co-operative way for generating self-employment and income. All of them, in the age group of 21 to 26 years, with little formal education, are engaged in making a living through skills they acquired without any specific planning or training. For instance, Santosh is a potter making small clay idols for festivals, Ajit is in the business of supplying cable connections, Sanjay is a ward boy in a Pune hospital, and Ganesh is a worker in a nearby packaging company. Four others are in the business of photography; three own/rent studios and one operates from his home.

PART TWO: YOUTH DEVELOPING CO-OPERATIVES *127*

It began when Nitin Shinde became fascinated with photography while still in his teenage years. He learned the skills from an experienced photographer in the village who owned the only photo studio. He nurtured his talent and expanded it into a business venture. He taught his elder brother and two friends the required skills. They too wanted to develop their skills into a business but did not know exactly how. Any idea they had was foiled because of the problem of procuring capital and finance. Their scale of operation was small, but their hurdle was a real one: how to secure sufficient funds to buy or even rent the equipment needed: namely, a still camera, a video camera, rolls of film, a place for the studio and funds for their day-to-day needs?

> The youngsters saw the women from their families participating in these SHGs, starting a credit co-operative and borrowing from their self-saved funds for meeting contingency needs – like finance for raw materials or even for such general household needs as health services and house repairs.

The solution to their problem came from an unexpected quarter. Rajiv Shinde noticed his mother's role in a women's Self Help Group that was being promoted as part of a rural poverty alleviation programme of the government, called the Swarnajayanti Grameen Swarojgar Yojana (SGSY). This scheme, limited to women, was based on using a group or co-operative model to enable women to save and generate adequate funds to pursue income-generating activities. The youngsters saw the women from their families participating in these SHGs, starting a credit co-operative and borrowing from their self-saved funds for meeting contingency needs – like finance for raw materials or even for such general household needs as health services and house repairs. They also saw the well functioning SHGs get a bank loan to further expand their income generating activities. They witnessed the results of these activities: namely, expansion of individual businesses, easing of financial crunches and overall better economics of the

MEMBERS OF THE CO-OPERATIVE

household. This inspired them to start their own credit co-operative. The question now was: how to proceed?

They first tried to find out if the government had a similar scheme for men or youth. They did not find any, but undeterred, they decided to proceed on their own. With the help of the social worker, who visited the village regularly for the women's group, they started the "Utkarsh Purush Bachat Gat" on the 12th of December 2003. Initially, there were 15 potential youth members, but five of them were dropped and only the present 10 were retained. This was because the five members were not in agreement with the majority about the structure of the co-operative, and the existing members were clear that all members should share similar goals for the co-operative to be successful.

Having established a credit co-operative, with a President and Secretary in place, they started to meet monthly and the business of saving began in earnest. Although the members lacked the skills and experience to put forth a clear vision and mission statement, they were clear about the purpose of their co-operative. They came together to address their individual needs for capital, working capital and/or personal expenses. They contributed Rs. 100 monthly and continued to save for the first five months. These savings were deposited in the Kedgaon branch of the "Pune District Madhyavarti Sahakari Bank Ltd". Members could take out loans after six months of savings, but loans were not sanctioned easily: demanders had to satisfy the group about the extent of the need and their repayment capacity. In the first year, three loans of Rs. 1500 were given to three members; a farmer who used it to buy fertilizers; a photographer who bought a still camera, and a member who needed funds to help buy a second-hand video camera. An interest rate of two percent per month was charged for the use of the funds.

> These small loans have helped the co-operative members expand their businesses, not only monetarily, but also in terms of mutual support, as the members are able to support each other in times of need.

Why did these young men not approach the bank directly for the required funds? To this question, all of them gave the same vehement answers: namely, that approaching a bank involves a lot of procedures, they would have to provide collateral, and, their requirements for working capital were small and recurrent, not worth the expenses and effort of approaching a bank. And finally, their credit co-operative was a much better way because they could interact with friends while receiving the financial help they needed.

These small loans have helped the co-operative members expand their businesses, not only monetarily, but also in terms of mutual support, as the members are able to support each other in times of need. Since four members are involved in providing photographic services, they never refuse any assignment that comes to any of them, even if it is at a far off place (e.g., for video shooting a marriage). They co-operate, rather than compete amongst themselves, to service such orders. The other members too are doing quite well in their respective occupations.

Sarah Groot, Uganda
Sarah Groot has been involved with co-operatives since she was a child. At fourteen, she attended the Co-operative Young Leaders Program which led her to take a more active role in the co-op sector. She has worked for St. Willibrord's Community Credit Union and worked with the Ontario Co-operative Associa- tion. Sarah graduated from the University of Guelph with a degree in Interna- tional Development and is currently working as a CCA intern in Uganda. She was the recipient of Ontario Co-op's 2004 Youth Leadership Spirit Award.

12

THE BUYOBE
YOUTH

Produce and Marketing Co-operative

Sarah Groot

Date of Incorporation: November 2003

Membership: 110 members, both males and females between the ages of thirteen and twenty-eight.

Activity: Sustainable income generating activities like beekeeping, fish farming and agriculture as well as HIV/AIDS awareness and sensitization.

Organization Form: Produce and Marketing Co-op

Area Served: Buyobe sub-county (containing 48 villages) Eastern Uganda

Co-op Story: In the Beginning

Our co-operative was formed in the Buyobe sub-county of Eastern Uganda to meet the needs of rural youth facing unemployment and systemic poverty. We held meetings and seminars to address the problems they faced. We decided to form a youth community-based organisation. We were specifically concerned about inadequate levels of technical, business and entrepreneurial skills; the inability to access and accumulate investment capital; the limited markets for products and services; and the high prevalence of HIV/AIDS among young people.

Becoming a Co-op

It wasn't until after the Uganda Co-operative Alliance (UCA) began working with our group as part of their Youth Economic Empowerment through Co-operatives (YEECO) project, that we decided to become a co-op. We chose the co-op model because it is the most appropriate form of business under which youth can obtain collective, as well as individual, services on a sustainable basis.

Before forming our co-op we had to learn many concepts, such as what a co-op is, how to start a co-op, advantages of a co-op, types of co-ops, how to register a co-op, leadership and management roles, rights and responsibilities of members, and accountability. Our advice to others is to seek information before starting a co-op.

We liked the co-op model because it is member-owned, used and controlled: in other words, the members have full authority over it. Some of the specific benefits of adopting the co-op model are: youth learn to work together and learn from each other through sharing experiences; they are offered opportunities for capacity building and skill improvement, and, most importantly, they can elect their own leaders.

DRAMA GROUP PERFORMING

A Focus on Youth

Old men with coffee and cotton dominate the existing co-ops in terms of membership, leadership and governance. This was unattractive to the youth because our views and needs weren't being considered. Now that we are specifically an organization of youth, members are finding it easier to openly discuss their problems and needs among fellow youth, and we are learning how to present ourselves without shyness through participatory discussions.

Organisational Structure & Governance

We are following a model that is suggested in the Co-operative Statute of 1991 and the 1992 Co-operative Regulations by the Registrar Commission for Co-operatives. Members of our co-op elect the board at their annual General Assembly. There are five to nine people on the Board, including a Chairperson, a Vice Chairperson, a Treasurer, a Secretary and Committee Members. At least four members of the Board have to be female youth.

One of the ways that members can get involved is to volunteer to help with the activities of the co-op. They benefit from volunteering because of the skills they develop and the opportunities for learning that occur. They can also win awards and bonuses. They can be good examples for others and they might get elected to the board or to a committee.

Because our co-operative operates in 48 villages, a vast area, we have established information agents, responsible for informing all our members about the co-op activities.

Our Goals

Our vision is to create an inclusive atmosphere for youth empowerment and participation in sustainable development. Our mission is to do through self-help, volunteerism, responsibility and co-ordination.

Our goals for the co-op are, in the short term, to empower youth with skills to manage their business, allow participatory discussions among them, decrease youth illiteracy about HIV/AIDS, and encourage gender equality in the co-op's activities. In the long term, we hope to decrease the number of youth in poverty and unemployment; increase the number of youth in agriculture as a business; and reduce the number of youth infected by the HIV/AIDS pandemic.

Measuring Success

We will measure our success in reaching these goals by material indicators such as number of items, tones of produce, number of members, etc. These indicators have

MEMBERS MEETING IN THE CO-OP OFFICE

specific, measurable units, and they have a time frame. In addition, we will also measure our progress by the level of member satisfaction with the co-operative. To measure the success of our social change objectives like gender equality, we can look at the number of female youth in the co-operative or in schools, but this is not enough. We rely on group discussion and consensus among our members to judge the level of change. Many members have to be involved and contribute in the participatory planning so that suitable indicators can be established.

Benefits to the Members

As a result of forming our co-op, people now appreciate the advantages of co-operation. Community members and young farmers are getting and appreciating agricultural training on different crops and animals, training that would have been difficult to get as individuals. Farmers in our community now have access to market information and are able to more advantageously market their products and services to potential buyers. Our co-op is also helping to educate people on topics of special interest by organizing small study circle groups. Finally, people are learning about and appreciating the benefits of saving, which is aiding their development.

Community Outreach

One of the major problems facing youth and our community is the high rate of infection by HIV/AIDS. Our co-op has been very active in sponsoring events to educate people on HIV/AIDS. The main way we do this is through music, dance and drama presentations in our communities.

Funding

Our co-op started with available land and labour. We required funding to buy materials, such as equipment for fish farming. We got some funding through fundraising ceremonies, proposal writing, grants from friends, and membership recruitment. However, a lack of sufficient funds to support our activities remains the main threat to our co-operative.

Based on our experiences, we think that government and Non-Government Organisations wishing to support youth co-operatives should fund youth trained in business, entrepreneurial and technical skills. Such youth need funds for seed capital instead of just training them and leaving them to sleep with their skills. Youth don't have seed capital or investment capital to start up what they have been trained to do. At the very least, they should be given funds in terms of loans so they can venture into business.

MEMBERS OF THE BOARD SHOWING OFF THE ACHIEVEMENTS OF THE CO-OP: HONEY THEY HAVE PRODUCED AND PACKAGED, AN AWARD WON FOR THEIR HIV/AIDS SENSITIZATIONS, AND FISH FROM THEIR FISHPOND

PHOTO OF CO-OP MEETING, 1940

HOUSE OWNED BY THE CO-OP IN THE 1940S

13

Student
HOUSING CO-OPERATIVES
in North America

Jim Jones, United States of America
Jim Jones is the Executive Director of the North American Students of Cooperation in Ann Arbour, the United States.

Jim Jones

In the years after the end of the American Civil War, many colleges and universities were opening their doors to women for the first time. Almost all students were men, and almost all lived in rooming houses near the campuses. There was very little housing provided by the universities, and women had a very hard time finding housing in such a male-dominated environment.

In 1871, in Evanston, Illinois, located just north of Chicago, a group of wealthy women decided to do something about the housing problems of the girls who were studying at a small teaching college in their community. They founded the Women's Educational Aid Association and in 1872 purchased a house that they called College Cottage. Six young women students lived there with a matron and a teacher, keeping costs low by doing their own cooking and cleaning. This group continued in different locations until 1968 – nearly 100 years – and was the first of what came to be known as student housing co-operatives.

These early efforts were not co-operatives in the sense that we now use the word. The word "co-op" meant shared work rather than user ownership and control. The women of the Aid Association owned the building and made the rules, as was true for nearly all later "co-ops" owned by alumni, universities or others who sought to help students by providing low cost housing. Indeed, some of these residences came to be known as scholarship halls, which might be a more truthful term. Regardless of what they were called, however, these groups all stressed self-help, and over time became a working model for affordable, non-profit student housing.

> And so it was, all over the United States. Groups of students banded together, formed co-operative corporations and either rented houses or, in some cases, purchased property.

In the 1930s, as the Great Depression hit hard on college campuses, students went hungry and often had to drop out of school. They needed a way to control costs, and housing was one of the biggest expenses for nearly everyone.

In 1942, Laia Hanau, a student at the University of Michigan, wrote a fictional novel about a student co-op during the Depression, called *Two Dollar House*. In her forward, she said:

> Some of the universities and colleges got behind us. In the Western States, in the Middle West, in California, Iowa, Oklahoma, Michigan, Ohio, they turned over unused buildings for conversion into co-operative dormitories; they built co-operative living quarters for us. We governed ourselves, we did our own cleaning, we bought our own food, we hired head chefs and worked under them, we established our own central eating kitchens. We put in four to six hours of work a week; and we lived on $15-20 a month. Seven years ago we formed the National Committee on Student Co-operatives, and we became a branch of the Co-operative League of America.
>
> Sixty-eight colleges and universities wanted us to stay, so they helped establish co-operative housing units for us. Twenty-one colleges and universities wanted us to go, so we established our own.[1]

And so it was, all over the United States. Groups of students banded together, formed co-operative corporations and either rented houses or, in some cases, purchased property. They were wildly successful in some places, although they drew mixed reactions from the college administrators.

The idea for starting a co-op came from a variety of sources. In the 1930s, one co-op began when a college president invited a group of poor students to eat with his family. At another school, a sociology professor helped a group of boys rent a deserted, broken down house. Agricultural co-ops helped to start several student housing co-operatives in the Midwest, while in Berkeley, the university YMCA lent a hand.

Today some of the older, college-owned "co-ops" still survive, but they are decreasing in number every year. At the same time, student-owned and operated co-ops

---

1   *Two Dollar House*, Laia Hanau, published by the Inter-Cooperative Council at the University of Michigan, Ann Arbor, Michigan. pg. iii.

are growing. The largest is in Berkeley, California, where the University Student Cooperative Association was started with a single house in 1933. There are now 1,200 student members in the co-op, living in twenty-two buildings worth many millions of dollars.

The smallest student co-ops have only five to fifteen members, often in rented houses. Some of these are started every year, often by graduate students who lived in co-ops elsewhere.

While all co-ops strive to own their property, it's not easy to convince a bank to loan thousands of dollars to a group of transient students with no track record. Perhaps the wonder is that any succeed at all. But students have found ways to purchase property for over 70 years now, and that ownership base is growing every year.

Through their association, the North American Students of Cooperation (NASCO), the student co-ops have supported one another through education, training, consulting and assistance with new purchases and refinancing.

> Student co-ops are somewhat different from family housing co-ops. The high turnover in a student community results in a great emphasis on participation and intense involvement to hold the group together.

Student co-ops are somewhat different from family housing co-ops. The high turnover in a student community results in a great emphasis on participation and intense involvement to hold the group together. The defining characteristics of student housing co-operatives in North America are:

- **Community.** There is an old co-op saying that people join for low cost and stay because of community. This is a vital element for student co-operatives because of high turnover. If there is no strong community, the members will not feel that it is important to do their work, pay their money and in general act as trustees for a building that they will pass on to the next generation. This sense of community is gained through (a) shared housework, which means that everyone contributes and works together for the better of the whole; (b) shared meals, which help people to know one another; and (c) group activities, from house meetings to parties.

- **Low cost.** While the co-ops may be only slightly less expensive than other rental units when they begin, they become increasingly affordable over time. The lower initial cost is achieved by (a) shared work, including everything from cooking and cleaning to minor maintenance work, accounting and bill paying; (b) collective buying of food and supplies; (c) shared facilities, such as kitchen appliances, phone, television, computer internet connections, etc.; and (d) density, with each person simply using less space than they would in traditional apartments. More savings are achieved over time because the property is not bought and sold, while the surrounding privately owned properties change hands at ever-rising prices.

- **Control.** For most students, living in a co-op is their first experience with home ownership, without rules from their parents, the university or a landlord. This is a tremendous responsibility, and they learn quickly. Some become leaders and are elected to officer positions, while others only take part through the meetings in which policy decisions are made. But their control is real, and they rise to the challenge.

Because of the intense, living-learning experience of a group housing co-operative, many members develop close bonds that last a lifetime. Moreover, they come to see the co-op as more than just a place to live while in school. They gain a sense of empowerment and learn the value of group action and democratic decision making.

Perhaps this sense of empowerment was best expressed by Richard Shuey, a member of a Congress House at the University of Michigan from 1938-1942, who wrote: *"The greatest thing about cooperative living is that if you don't like it, you can change it."*[2]

DIGGING IN THE GARDEN TOGETHER

---

2   *The Cooperator,* a publication of the Inter-Cooperative Council at the University of Michigan, March, 1939

Katende Billy and Sarah Groot, Uganda
Katende Billy is the Chairperson of the Kiyoola Youth Development Association.
He is twenty-two years old and lives in Mukono District, Uganda.

Sarah Groot has been involved with co-operatives since she was a child. At fourteen, she attended the Co-operative Young Leaders Program which led her to take a more active role in the co-op sector. She has worked for St. Willibrord's Community Credit Union and worked with the Ontario Co-operative Association. Sarah graduated from the University of Guelph with a degree in International Development and is currently working as a CCA intern in Uganda. She was the recipient of Ontario Co-op's 2004 Youth Leadership Spirit Award.

14

KIYOOLA

Youth Development Co-operative

Katende Billy and Sarah Groot

Name of Co-operative: Kiyoola Youth Development Co-operative

Date of Formation: August 2002

Membership: The group is for both male and female youth, aged from 12-35 years; we now have 112 youth members

Activity: The co-op brings together youth to undertake drama, HIV/AIDS sensitization, agriculture, and other activities.

Organization Form: Worker's Producer Co-op

Area Served: Kiyoola sub-county, Eastern Uganda

Background

The paramount motives that led to the establishment of our co-operative were the desire to abolish unemployment among young people and to develop different talents in the youth.

Vision/Purpose/Goals

By the year 2009, Kiyoola Youth Development Co-operative will be in a position to provide services to all categories of young people in the areas of education, mobilization and employment, thereby boosting income-generating activities that will make the community a better place in which to live. This group meets the needs and aspirations of young people through hard work and being creative in income generating activities.

The benefits of organizing the co-operative to the local communities are that it helps to create income-generating activities among youth, encourages them to develop their talents, promotes agriculture in the wasted areas in our communities, and combats drug use among young people.

AGRICULTURAL ACTIVITIES INCLUDE: DRYING PINEAPPLE

CO-OPERATIVE SOLUTIONS ARE EMPHASISED AT WORKSHOPS

Starting the Co-op

The people involved in starting the co-operative were the board members and the community development officer of our sub-county, who gave us guidance. Some of the pioneer members of the co-op had formed a group for youth after being trained under the Promoting Children and Youth (PCY) of the Ministry of Gender, Labour and Social Development. It was from within this PCY group that the co-op was built.

The resources that were available to begin with were hired land and study materials. More funding is needed so that the co-operative can buy its own land and develop it by cultivating crops. The co-op also needs to purchase instruments for the drama group, and to support co-op members with resources as they develop their talents. The co-op would like to support some of its pioneer members as they pursue studies in social work so they can further help the community.

The group has been supported in its development through both private and community resources. It is also part of the Youth Economic Empowerment through Co-operatives (YEECO) sponsored by the Uganda Co-operative Alliance. YEECO trainers and staff have assisted the group to develop, by helping to improve discipline among group members and bringing them some services like trainings about HIV/AIDS and agriculture.

Some of the obstacles that the co-operative is encountering in its development are:

- The lack of funds,
- the lack of good markets for the products,
- the lack of youth trained in development,
- the lack of members trained in how to run a co-operative, and
- a lack of trainers to develop drama activities and other talents.

Future Plans

We have a business plan in place and are working harder to find our dream. We have working sites where different activities are done in order to improve on the standard of living of our members. We also have a drama group, which has done great work in sensitizing and mobilizing about HIV/AIDS, healthy lifestyles, sanitation and social behaviours. All of these activities are sources of revenue for our co-operative.

In the near future, we need to offer different training programmes and seminars concerning savings and credit, social life, Health (HIV/AIDS), and business practice. We need to have more income generating activities to add to those we already have, and we need to improve on the quality and the quantity of the crop yield in the co-op. We hope to help fellow youth with HIV/AIDS if we earn good funds. To help our co-operative grow in the long term, we are hoping to extend to other areas and recruit more projects to earn more income. We can also get more resources by asking for donations and funds from different organisations.

Lessons Learned

To start, organize and run a co-operative is not simple work. It requires the following: participation, collaboration, creativity, active participants, assistance, tolerance, wit, and flexibility. The advice we could give to others is to be aware of the above-mentioned principles and to be aware of the challenges because the world isn't straight.

Suroto, Indonesia

Suroto joined the General Soedirman University student co-operative (now "SOEDIRMAN" Co-operative) in 1997 (Chairman for the period 2000-2001 and 2001-2003). With other youth activists he helped create the Institute for Co-operative Studies and Development (LePPeK) in 2003. He has been its director since its formation.

15
Indonesian
YOUTH CO-OPERATIVES
and the Changed Environment

Suroto

Introduction

Co-operatives in developing countries have different characteristics from co-operatives in developed countries, differences explained by social structures, social systems, economics and politics. In developed countries, most co-operatives operate as autonomous and independent institutions. In some developing countries like Indonesia, governments play dominant roles and co-operatives at the local and national level have the tendency to be used as government tools.

The Indonesian people are also still largely unaware of the co-operative movement. Only about 27 million of the country's 215 million people in Indonesia are members of the 103,000 co-operatives spread all over the country (Minister of Cooperatives: 2003). Moreover, many of the co-operatives reported are, in fact, not now in operation and many do not follow the co-operative principles in their operating practices. Top-down management dominates too many co-operatives and member participation is weak and inefficiently managed: they do business like conventional companies, being only concerned with profits. Competitively, some co-operatives cannot compete with other forms of market companies. Unfortunately, there are also cases of corruption, fraud and manipulation that weaken people's trust in co-operatives.

> Top-down management dominates too many co-operatives and member participation is weak and inefficiently managed: they do business like conventional companies, being only concerned with profits.

This context, of course, affects the role of youth in the co-operative movement. Youth tend to see co-operatives as uninteresting organizations, and only a few take advantage of co-operative opportunities. We can see this from the weak participation of youth in the national co-operative movement. Even the minority of youth who are active in some sectors of co-operation do not always show a strong commitment to the continuity of co-operatives. The gap between the youth and co-operation in Indonesia seems to be quite large.

Youth Cooperative Organization and Its Achievements

There are approximately five million youth involved in the Indonesian co-operative movement (Kuncoro: 2004). This is a small percentage, if we compare it with the number of youth in general, which is approximately 90.3 million people[1]. The numbers of youth in co-operatives in Indonesia includes those who join in many kinds of co-operative sectors, such as credit unions, village co-operative units, farming co-operatives,

MEMBERS OF AN INDONESIAN YOUTH CO-OPERATIVE

diary co-ops and others, as well as those who are engaged in co-ops exclusively for young people, such as university student co-operatives (Kopma's), student co-operatives (Kopsis's), and co-operatives for youth (Kopda's).

Those who are involved in many kinds of general co-operative organisations, like credit unions, diary co-ops, and farming co-operatives, make only minor contributions. Their involvement has not been supported in co-operative policy: their activities and youth programmes receive minimum budget allocations. However, youth have been involved in some positive activities: they have been enlisted as education facilitators holding "Cow Expeditions" in diary co-ops, running competitions, and managing co-operative magazines. Generally, they have not been significantly involved in developing co-operative policy, though in some co-operatives they have created their own forum to help meet their needs.

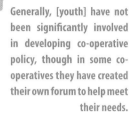

Generally, [youth] have not been significantly involved in developing co-operative policy, though in some co-operatives they have created their own forum to help meet their needs.

Young people active in exclusively youth co-operatives have succeeded in creating strong apex organisations at the local and national level. At the national level, youth co-operatives have formed many organisations, including the following:

- the Youth Co-operative Communication Body (BKPK), which is a youth co-operative organisation underneath the Board of Indonesian Co-operative (Dekopin);
- the Indonesian Youth Co-op (Kopindo's), which is a secondary youth co-operative in Indonesia;
- the Indonesian Student Co-operative Communication Forum (FKKMI), a network created by the university student co-operatives.

At the local level, there are other organisations:

- the Yogyakarta Student Co-op Union (HKMY);
- the Semarang Student Co-operative Association (Akomas);
- the Jakarta Student Co-operative Association (Akukopma); and
- the Bandung Student Co-operative Association (Asbikom).

The co-operatives run by young people at the local level operate a number of businesses, including mini markets, copy centres, cafes, phone shops, and student dormitories. Others run savings and loan services, computer courses, and foreign language courses as well as seminars, co-operative education and training programmes, and management training. University student co-operatives are not always able to develop their programmes as they would wish to do because they are dependent on their "landlord", the university, for the facility in which they exist.

University Students Co-operatives and The Discourse of Change

Currently, there are 139 university student co-operatives[2]. The first co-operative of this type was established in 1974, as "Bumi Siliwangi" IKIP Bandung (now called University of Indonesia Education (UPI) Bandung). According to Darsono (2002), a second co-operative was soon established because of efforts to "muzzle" the voice of university students demanding social and political change during the 1970s. Some students charge, therefore, that university student co-operatives act as servants of the capitalist state and only develop entrepreneurial skills helpful to people who wish to work in the capitalist sector.

A report on six big university student's co-operatives in Indonesia prepared by the Canadian Co-operative Association (CCA) in 1996 is also critical, albeit for somewhat different reasons:

> We didn't see the service provided by these co-operative as instruments of democracy or change, but rather as a means of satisfying tangible or consumable needs. Perhaps we didn't see these co-operatives as a part of something larger, such as a consumer co-operative movement.[3]

The trend of establishing university student co-operatives continued until 1995. Twelve percent were established between the years 1975 to 1979, 68 percent were established between the years 1980 to 1986 and 21 percent were established between the years 1986 to 1995. Sixty-eight percent of university co-operatives have automatic or top down membership – students automatically become members when they register – and only 32 have voluntary membership (Darsono: 2003). Recently, though, more co-operatives have been becoming voluntary and a few are opening themselves as public co-operatives, following the ordinary consumer co-op model.

> Some students charge, therefore, that university student co-operatives act as servants of the capitalist state and only develop entrepreneurial skills helpful to people who wish to work in the capitalist sector.

The effects of these changes were evident at a recent Seminar and Workshop of Indonesia University Student Co-operative. The forms of university co-operatives represented included:

- university students co-operatives with memberships open only to university students;

- university student co-operatives that still keep the name but open memberships to the community; and

- university students co-operatives that have become open to the public and have changed their names

---

2   The valid statistic number until this paper is compile hasn't been found, according to the Office of Minister of Co-operative there are about 500 primary co-operatives. Meanwhile the data that writer used is university student co-operative listed to be the member of FKKMI until 2004
3   See CCA : INCODAP Co-operative Youth Programs : technical Co-operant Report, Study Mission to Indonesia, CCA, 1996, not published

Principle Problems

There are a number of general reasons why co-operatives are not fully meeting the needs of youth in Indonesia.

- Youth do not realize the importance of co-operatives.
- Co-operative organizers do not recognise the importance of youth involvement.
- Co-operatives do not present an attractive image to youth.
- The average education level of co-operative youth is low, and some still have to finish their school.
- Co-operatives do not have the capacity to give youth economic benefits.

Co-operatives that exist to meet the needs of youth, such as university student co-operatives and student co-operatives, face some specific problems:

- In many, membership is still automatic and member interest is low;
- The participation level of members in co-operatives is still low with the average of less than 50%;
- The organizing of resources is difficult and management pattern is not sufficiently professional;
- High dependency upon "landlords";
- Weak communications with the membership;
- Insufficient management education and training;
- Weak co-operative network;

SOME STUDENT CO-OPERATORS

- Limited direct benefit from membership;

- Lack of sensitivity from the "co-operative elites";

- The discourse of "Campus Autonomy" is considered by some leaders of the universities as an effort to take away the business opportunities of university student co-operatives; and

- A lack of understanding that university student co-operatives are an important part of universities.

Conclusion and Recommendations

The role of youth in co-operatives still seems small and young people lack influence in the making of key decisions. The co-operative movement in Indonesia needs to formulate a vision that promotes youth involvement and those leading general co-operatives need to be more responsive to the changes that surround them.

I recommend the following changes in order to empower youth in co-operatives:

- Develop more effective youth involvement strategies;

- Change the general attitudes towards youth through workshops, seminars, and publications;

- Develop budgetary support for programmes leading to greater youth involvement;

- Develop stronger youth networks at local, national or even international level through the use of facilitators and youth camps;

- Develop workshops to promote youth creativity and employment opportunities based on co-operative entrepreneurship;

- Ensure the continuity of youth programmes in the co-operative movement thereby assuring co-operative development in the future;

- Increase the opportunities for youth empowerment in the Indonesian economy and the co-operative movement; and

- Co-operatives involved in youth empowerment must recognize that they will have to adapt themselves to a rapidly changing environment.

Stephen Kirk, Canada
Stephen Kirk is a member of Organic Planet Worker Co-operative.

16

Organic Planet
WORKER CO-OP

Stephen Kirk

Organic Planet Worker Co-op opened in Winnipeg, Manitoba, Canada, during May 2003 at a location that had been home to a retail food co-op for the previous 25 years. When that business was closing, the Community Economic Development Manager at a local credit union (Assiniboine) stepped in to develop a succession plan. If a core group could be formed and a viable business plan created, then the credit union would provide support for a worker co-op to purchase and run the business.

Most of the founding members were young people with some experience working in an organic store, but little or none in running one. Others had previous work experience in other Winnipeg worker co-ops. The five founding members contributed almost two months of volunteer time working towards a proposal that the credit union could support. This was quite a tense time, as people worried about paying their rents, and whether or not they would be able to make a new job for themselves.

SEED Winnipeg, an anti-poverty agency that works by helping individuals and groups start small businesses and save money for future goals, helped form the business plan. Another organisation essential to the creation of OPWC was

> *If a core group could be formed and a viable business plan created, then the credit union would provide support for a worker co-op to purchase and run the business.*

ORGANIC PLANET STORE IN WINNIPEG

the Canadian Worker Co-op Federation, which provided loans of start-up capital. The CWCF continues to be a valuable forum for networking with other worker co-ops, both in our hometown and across the country.

Today, Organic Planet Worker Co-op has nine staff and seven members. They operate a lively little store that sells organic produce, organic groceries, some health and beauty products; it also operates an organic/vegetarian deli.

For new staff, there is a nine month probationary period. After successful completion, they are offered the opportunity to join the co-op buy purchasing a share. Shares cost $500, which may be paid over time through paycheque deductions. As a worker co-op, our raison d'etre is to provide good jobs for our members.

Whenever possible, Organic Planet purchases from local producers and from other co-ops. Fair trade and certified organic are preferred, as are smaller, more independent suppliers. A large variety of bulk foods helps to limit wasteful packaging. We help customers connect with the sources of their food by offering store tours and by emphasizing our support for local environmental causes. We also believe it is important that the members have a good understanding of where the food we purchase and sell comes from. We have had meetings at various organic farms and tours of our suppliers' businesses to help give them this understanding.

Organic Planet Worker Co-op is now nearly two years old, and operates without a deficit. All founding members still work in the business, although for near minimum wages. This is possible for young people, but one day the co-op will have to provide pay that will enable members to support families. Our challenge now is to tend the business well, so that our dividends will grow, thereby making our jobs more sustainable.

MEMBERS MAX AND EMILY WITH SOME ORGANIC PRODUCE

PART THREE:

Co-operatives Encouraging Youth Involvement

Historically, the co-operative movement has always demonstrated an interest in communicating its messages and providing its benefits to young people. The Rochdale Pioneers, shortly after their store was opened, recognized what they could do on behalf of young people and formed a youth study club for them. In 1853, as their Society prospered, they proposed that 10% of their surpluses (or profits) should be allocated for educational activities, many of them for the young. For better or worse, the UK Registrar opposed such generosity but agreed to a lesser commitment to 2½ per cent of their surpluses, still a significant percentage that few co-ops today can match.

Education of young people, in fact, became one of the key aspects of the co-operative movement as it emerged in industrializing Europe in the nineteenth century, a carry-over from the influences of the Enlightenment and the thoughts of Robert Owen; the result of the impact of such thinkers as St. Simon, Charles Fourier, Bishop Nikolai Grundtvig, Freidrich Raiffeisen, Luigi Luzzatti, Alphonse Desjardins, and Charles Gide.

The commitment to education, broadly conceived – a commitment that went far beyond "competency training" – was a hallmark of the consumer movement as it emerged in the United Kingdom and most other countries in the late nineteenth and early twentieth centuries, sparking the formation of co-operative colleges, training institutes, and adult education programmes. As some cases in this book demonstrate, that tradition still flourishes.

The community-based co-operative banks, such as credit unions, have often had special programmes to encourage youth to save and to understand the value of thrift. That, too, as other cases demonstrate, is still evident. Many rural co-operatives around the world have developed youth clubs and sponsored a wide range of youth activities aimed at teaching good agricultural practices and at encouraging young people to stay on the farms. Many housing co-operatives have special educational programmes for the children in their midst. The worker co-operative movement, as the forgoing section has shown, has been arguably the most open to youth involvement and empowerment…and young people have been easily attracted to the idea of worker co-operative, perhaps signalling the beginnings of a "golden age" in that movement's development. Less evident in the following, but ubiquitous within the movement, all kinds of co-operatives have developed scholarship and bursary programmes to help young people with their academic and technical studies.

The case studies that follow give examples of youth activities sponsored by various co-operative organisations, though one can also see ways in which government involvement is also significant. As among other age groups, co-operatives among youth are a reflection of many trends, pressures and circumstances in a society at a given time. Little in the co-operative world, young or old, happens in isolation.

The Editors

SCHOOL CO-OPERATIVE TOURISM PARTICIPANTS LISTENING ATTENTIVELY DURING A STUDY VISIT TO TERATAK ZA'ABA, NEGERI SEMBILAN HOSTED BY PENDETA ZA'ABA SECONDARY SCHOOL CO-OPERATIVE LTD

ROYAL PROF UNGKU A AZIZ PRESENTING PRIZES TO LIKAS SECONDARY SCHOOL CO-OPERATIVE LTD, SECOND-PLACE WINNERS OF NATIONAL SCHOOL CO-OPERATIVE DAY 2004

Rahaiah Baheran, Malaysia
Rahaiah is ANGKASA's Vice-President since 1994. She serves as Chairperson of ANG-
KASA's Education and Women's Development Committee. She is also the Chairperson
of the ICA Regional Women's Committee for Asia and the Pacific and a Board Member
of the ICA Gender Equality Committee. As the first chairperson of the ICA Regional
Women's Committee for Asia Pacific, Rahaiah has been on the ICA Board since 1996.

ANGKASA:

Its Role in the Development of School Co-operatives in Malaysia

Rahaiah Baheran

Name of Co-operative: The co-operative is called the National Co-operative Organisation of Malaysia (ANGKASA).

Date of Incorporation: 12 May 1971.

Membership: The organisation serves 3031 co-operatives and 5.3 million members (as of January 2005). Of this total, 1376 are school co-operatives, comprising 1.36 million members.

Activity: Apex organisation of the Malaysian co-operative movement, provides educational and support services.

Organisational Form: National Apex Co-operatives.

Area Served: The organisation serves co-operatives in Malaysia.

Introduction

The First Malaysian Co-operative Congress in 1953 passed a resolution urging the Government to set up co-operatives in schools to inculcate the co-operative model among school children. The project took off in 1968 with nine schools being selected for the pilot project. Since then, the number has increased by more than 150-fold and confidence in the school co-operative movement has grown tremendously.

The school co-op is recognized and accepted as a co-curriculum activity in Malaysia by the Government, which sees it as an important and meaningful activity, especially for secondary school students. The government formalized its support for the national programme in the country's Education Act (1961) and the National Education Policy.

The members of the co-ops are mainly students ranging from 12 to 17 years of age, a particularly good age for people to be involved in such activities, a very valuable timeframe to introduce co-operative principles and values to the youths. The Government acknowledges that, through co-operative movement, the young students could be developed, among others, as responsible and independent persons, whilst being given opportunity for leadership and business exposure.

WISMA UNGKU A AZIZ AT KELANA JAYA, OPERATIONAL SINCE 1997 IN ITS OWN BUILDING.

THE PARTICIPANTS OF THE NATIONAL SCHOOL CO-OPERATIVE DAY 2004 AT ANGKASA'S AUDITORIUM

ANGKASA

The National Co-operative Organisation of Malaysia (ANGKASA) is recognized by the Malaysian government as the national apex body of co-operative organisations. It was registered in May, 1971. The membership of ANGKASA is currently 3,031 co-operatives at the primary, secondary and tertiary levels, including school co-operatives. All told, 1,376 of the 1,472 school co-operatives in existence are members of ANGKASA.

ANGKASA was formed to meet the following objectives:

- To unite and represent the Malaysian Co-operative Movement at the national and international level;
- To disseminate and propagate the co-operative concept and principles through education and publicity; and
- To assist co-operatives in the proper running and management of the organisations by providing advice, education and other necessary services.

The school co-operative movement in Malaysia is highly regarded internationally for its activities and its achievements. It has been highlighted a number of times during the International Co-operative Alliance (ICA) General and Regional Assemblies. However, its success would not be accomplished without the joint effort and mutual understanding between the Ministry of Education and ANGKASA in developing the co-operative movement in the schools.

ANGKASA is headed by the National Administrative Committee comprising fifteen elected officials: the President, the Deputy President, three Vice Presidents and ten State Committee Chairpersons.

Development of School Co-operative Movement

As an apex body, ANGKASA played an important role in promoting and develop co-operatives in schools. For ANGKASA, the best way to develop the movement is through education. Among the activities organized include:

- Administrative and Management Course;
- Annual Celebration of School Co-operative Day – State and National level;
- School Co-operative Tourism; and
- SEKKOP 123 (Accounting System).

A. Administrative and Management Course

Members and internal audit committee attend this course. The aim of the course is to equip board members and auditors with the knowledge and skills in managing their

MDM RAHAIAH BAHERAN WITH PARTICIPANTS OF SCHOOL CO-OPERATIVE TOURISM VISITING THE LANGUAGE MUSEUM, MALACCA

co-operative effectively. There are six modules in the course, which consists of the following:

- □ Understanding the Co-operative Identity Statement;
- □ Understanding the Co-operative's Financial Statement;
- □ Good Governance for Co-operative;
- □ Co-operative's Society's Law in Malaysia;
- □ Co-operative's Financial Management; and
- □ Rights and Responsibilities of Co-operative Board Members

B. Annual Celebration of School Co-operative Day

ANGKASA organized its first School Co-operative Day in 1995 and has held them every year since then. The annual event is divided into two categories, state and national level. It is a joint effort between ANGKASA, the Ministry of Education, State Education Departments and the Department of Co-operative Development of Malaysia. The events organized include the Quiz Competition, an Essay Writing Competition, and a Drawing Competition; it also features Seminars and a Petanque Tournament with themes related to co-operatives and their movement. The participation from the schools has been encouraging and the competition has garnered attention among school going children. The prizes awarded to Quiz and

SCENE AT THE KELANTAN STATE SCHOOL CO-OPERATIVE DAY'S PETANQUE COMPETITION. PETANQUE IS A TRADITIONAL FRENCH LAWN BALL GAME.

Petanque winners include a trip to visit co-operatives and universities in ASEAN countries. The winning participant in the Quiz competition is given the opportunity to experience first hand the co-operative movement around the world. Since 1995, the winners have been to Manchester (1995), Japan (1996, 2000, 2002, 2003), Sweden (1997), Thailand (1998), Canada (1999) and Korea (2001). All the expenses for this travel were borne by ANGKASA.

C. School Co-operative Tourism

The School Co-operative Tourism package introduced by ANGKASA differs from the packages by travel agencies. It emphasizes educational programmes rather then typical tourism and sightseeing. Currently being developed in selected schools in Peninsular Malaysia, it involves local co-operatives in two ways: they can organize tours for their members to visit other co-operatives, or they can host members from other co-operatives. In either event, the programme provides students with the opportunity to plan and to manage tourist packages. When a co-operative serves as a host, it will provide accommodation and organize the itinerary for the stay, including educational activities. The package is drawn up based on a local historical figure who has contributed to the development of Malaysia and includes a discussion on the figure and his or her contributions. The tour also includes a visit to historical sites in relating to the subject. ANGKASA provides training and guidance for this programme.

D. SEKKOP 123

ANGKASA developed an integrated accounting software programme – Membership, Accounting and Sales System, also known as SEKKOP 123 for school co-operatives. Introduced in 2001, it helps school co-operatives to manage their services better in the areas of sales transaction, stock control, registration of membership and accounting. ANGKASA makes the software available free of charge to school co-operatives. The advantage of having this software is that less time is needed for finalizing accounts and stock taking, thus helping teachers and students run the business efficiently.

Conclusion

ANGKASA plays a significant role in the development of school co-operatives. Guided by the co-operative principles and values, ANGKASA believes in providing a positive environment for school co-operatives to thrive in the country and for young people to learn about co-operatives and their effective management.

2

Federation of
Co-operative Agrarian
YOUTH CENTRES

Argentina

Date of Incorporation: September 1950

Membership: The Federation has over 600 associates. Their average age is 21 years old; most have secondary school education and approximately 30% have university education. The minimum age for joining the Federation is fourteen years.

Activities

The Federation's main activities are training young people and helping farm families improve their production methods. Through training, the Federation also tries to encourage the development of co-operative and technical entrepreneurial attitudes among youth. Though it is concerned that its young entrepreneurial members know about dairying, it also wants them to know about co-operatives in other sectors as well. The Federation believes that co-operativism is a social attitude: "you do not only learn to become a co-operativist at SanCor, but to be a co-operativist in any environment in which you participate".

The Federation promotes activities that will diversify manufacturing and make it possible to for young people to find work within their rural setting. Some of its most important production ventures are: the development of a forest nursery, a programme for the promotion of beekeeping, and a honey extraction room.

Organisational Form

The Federation is a non-governmental and non-profit organisation. It is open to children of producers who are members of the Dairy Farm Co-operatives associated with SanCor United Co-operatives Limited.

Service Area

The Federation is active within the provinces of Santa Fe, Córdoba, Entre Ríos, Buenos Aires and Santiago del Estero, the area known as the SanCor's milk basin. Its headquarters are in the province of Córdoba.

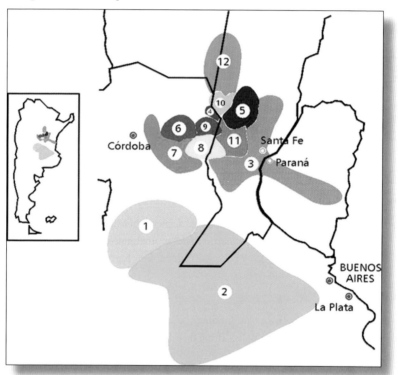

Antecedents / Context

The young rural people of the SanCor milk basin became interested in co-operativism during the 1940s, when the co-operative movement in the country was experiencing a boom. Young people began to meet daily at the San Cor Co-operative, where they

THE FEDERATION'S MISSION: TO TRAIN YOUNG RURAL CO-OPERATIVISTS BY PROVIDING THEM WITH KNOWLEDGE AND RESOURCES

delivered their products. They recognised the need for training in co-operative theory and principles, and very soon they began to organize themselves to meet that need. With the support of the Co-operative's executives, they formed the Co-operativist Agrarian Youth Organising Commission of the Zona SanCor. This Commission started spreading the idea and organising young dairy farmers in local Youth Centres.

In the 1950s there were limited educational resources, especially in the rural areas, and the Federation was organized in part to help meet this need. In addition to its functions of assisting to provide vocational training demand and understanding of co-operativist doctrine, the Federation helped organize people to provide important social services necessary for the well-being of rural families.

After 30 Youth Centres had been created, young people within the movement decided to form a second tier organisation and organized the Co-operativist Agrarian Youth Centres Zona SanCor, under the sponsorship of the Butter Factory SanCor. It was designated as the driving, co-ordinating, and guiding organisation for co-operativist agrarian youth within the dairy movement of SanCor.

Vision / mission

Our vision is "to be the organisation in the co-operative rural movement that trains and develops its young people socially, morally, and technically so that they can use the co-operative movement to pursue a better quality of life."

Our mission is "to train young rural co-operativists by providing them with knowledge and resources helpful in improving the productive process of their farm activities and in learning about the benefits of co-operative doctrine."

Goals

- To group, co-ordinate, and guide the Co-operativist Agrarian Youth Centres' present and future activities and to encourage their association with the Federation.

- To programme our cultural and organisational activities according to the tenets of co-operativism, thereby spreading the system's virtues, providing youth with technical information, and encouraging more efficient performance within the co-operatives' administration.

- To encourage diversified production and increased efficiency of the young people's work in rural operations.

- To promote participation by rural young people in zone activities.

- To systematically analyse rural life issues and farm work so as to help members achieve a better and more dignified way of life.

- To encourage the unification and integration of a national co-operativist agrarian youth movement.

- To promote cultural and athletic events for the recreation and relaxation of members at the Federated Youth Centres.

GROUP PHOTO OUTSIDE THE FEDERATION HEADQUARTERS

CO-OPERATORS HAVING SOME FUN IN THE SUN

Organisational Structure

The Zona SanCor is divided into 12 regional zones, each with a zonal youth centre. Each centre is associated with local youth centres.

The Board of Directors of the Federation, made up of 18 young people, the children of producers of SanCor United Co-operatives Limited, directs the affairs of the movement. Members of the Board represent the various youth centres as well, in some instances, independent youth commissions in the regional zones. The Board is made up of 12 permanent members, representing all the regional zones, along with four substitute members and two trustees. Each permanent member serves for three years and each substitute serves for one year. Each trustee is elected for one year and can be re-elected for one additional term.

The Board of Directors meets for two days each month. During the first day the Board members meet in committees to consider different issues and on the second day they meet to make decisions. All members work on a voluntary basis. Members have to be the children of a producer or an agriculture or livestock producer in order to join the Boards of Directors of the Federation or the Zonal Youth Centres. One must be between 21 and 36 years old to be a member of the Executive of the Youth Centres or the Federation.

Members at the local level are encouraged to participate because doing so will enable them to attend the annual general assembly, which brings together participants from all of the regional centres.

Links to the community

Through their work with the Federation, young people have been encouraged to establish bonds with other service co-operatives, universities, and such institutions as the National Institute of Farming Technology (INTA).

Resources

Activities are funded by income generated by the Federation through its productive activities, as well as financial support from SanCor and support from the communities in which local youth centres are active. Members' families also have made important contributions – and not just financial. Members are charged for services, usually on a cost recovery basis.

Future Plans

Plans for the future include strengthening the Rural Co-operativist Family and slowing down the rural exodus of young people. This objective will be achieved by encouraging economic activities that will allow young people to work close to the places in which they grew up. Activities that promote the interests of women are being emphasized in 2005.

NATIONAL GATHERING OF YOUTH CO-OPERATORS

Present Concerns

The co-op seeks to expand the possibilities for well-paying and satisfying work for members of rural families. One key concern is the problem of inter-generational succession, an historic issue of great importance in our country – and many other countries as well. An important part of this concern is the desire to create satisfactory work for young people on the farms and our co-op is trying to work with young co-operativists as they go through that process. In the case of those who are close to graduating from their schools, the Federation helps them to plan their future, taking into account their personal abilities and the probable viability of what they hope to do. The Federation offers technical and even financial support through its Programme of Sustainable Development.

In this sense, the SanCor Co-operative, and the co-operatives of the dairy sector linked to it, support the initiatives and projects young people propose and undertake. They encourage economic development within rural communities and help young people to become established through programmes of promotion, training, credit, technical assistance, and monitoring.

Message

The best advice for co-operativist youth and youth in general is that they need to become active and participate. "Youth is not future, it is present...if we organize we can become activists able to change the future." A way to encourage more young people to use the co-operative model to satisfy their economic and social needs would be to encourage participation within existing co-operatives. By being involved in the programmes meeting their interests and needs and by being willing and able to contribute their time and energy, they can make important contributions to the development of educational and developmental projects.

When young people are involved, the value of working together becomes more apparent. Governments and educational institutions should promote the teaching of co-operative education in all institutions so that young people can know the system and help it grow.

VANCITY SEEKS TO HELP CHILDREN LEARN ABOUT REAL-LIFE FINANCIAL ISSUES IN A FUN AND INTERESTING WAY

Erik Haensel, Canada
Erik Haensel is a researcher at the British Columbia Institute for Co-operative Studies registered in a History and Environmental Studies programme.

CULTIVATING DREAMS:

Vancity

helps youth meet their

financial goals

Erik Haensel

"Learning about money management is easy when you are having fun."

These encouraging words were spoken by a student who took part in the "PowerPlay Money Managers" programme at a school in the Vancouver area. The programme, sponsored by Vancity credit union, seeks to help children learn about real-life financial issues in a fun and interesting way.

Vancity is Canada's largest credit union, with $9.0 billion in assets, over 300,000 members, and 42 branches throughout Greater Vancouver, the Fraser Valley and Victoria. Vancity owns Citizens Bank of Canada, serving members across the country by telephone, ATM, and the Internet. Both Vancity and Citizens Bank are guided by a commitment to corporate social responsibility, and to improve the quality of life in the communities where members live and work. The PowerPlay Money Managers programme, is just one of many ways Vancity works to involve youth in co-operative financial planning.

With different approaches for different age groups, Vancity sponsors financial education programmes that are relevant to young children and senior high school students alike. By focusing first on helping students define financial components of their own goals, the Vancity programme helps students understand that using financial management skills can be an empowering process.

> **To involve elementary school children, Vancity has created an innovative Youth Credit Union system where students in grade six and seven function as bank tellers, office staff, and board members.**

To involve elementary school children, Vancity has created an innovative Youth Credit Union system where students in grade six and seven function as bank tellers, office staff, and board members. The other students, including students from earlier grades can then become members of these co-operatives and learn how to manage a bank account.

Through partnerships with local schools, the programme has expanded to include 19 youth credit unions serving more than 1,800 students across the Lower Mainland. Together, they've saved more than $850,000 – one loonie at a time.

The programme started in 1996 with the twin goals of teaching kids about savings and money management, while helping them to build their confidence, leadership and math skills. To date, it seems to be an extremely effective way to empower youth and teach them how to manage money to fit their dreams, rather than fitting their dreams into an unkempt financial situation.

> **By encouraging students to contemplate what would be involved in obtaining a car loan, planning effectively for post-secondary education or other tangible relevant goals, they empower students to set goals, and make positive choices that bring them closer to those goals.**

For older youth, Vancity has engaged PowerPlay Strategies Inc. (specialists in youth-oriented financial education) to offer a slightly different programme, but on the same principles of empowerment and encouragement. The PowerPlay Money Managers programme, which is designed for Grade 10 students, introduces relevant financial topics to students to help them build practical life skills.

By encouraging students to contemplate what would be involved in obtaining a car loan, planning effectively for post-secondary education or other tangible relevant goals, they empower students to set goals, and make positive choices that bring them closer to those goals.

Students learn about different methods of financial planning, including budgeting, dealing with loans, managing income, and investing. Further, students are encouraged to lead family discussions in order to integrate what they are learning into the lives of their families in a meaningful way.

Not only have students appreciated the useful and enjoyable nature of the projects, but teachers have found that teaching the program is rewarding as well. Marianne Marcario from Handsworth Secondary School comments:

This programme was easy to use, and it helped me achieve my goals with Planning 10. The engaging activities and group discussions activate the learning process. My students had fun exploring the world of finance, were presented with real-life situations and were inspired to take action at home.

In order to take their support of young adults one step further, Vancity has also sponsored the Generation Y Entrepreneurship programme, which was created by the Canadian Youth Business Foundation (CYBF). The Foundation, which is a national non-profit organization, provides resources, mentoring, and loans to youth aged eighteen to twenty-four. In the past, the Foundation has split its resources between support and loans, trying to balance financial opportunity for youth with the importance of long-term mentoring, and targeted skill training programmes. This is where Vancity came on board providing much needed loan capital to the programme and allowing the Foundation to free up resources to expand and further their existing support programmes. Engaging in the complex competitive global market place can be a daunting thought for many youth. But with the confidence and skill building combination provided by Vancity's "PowerPlay Money Managers" programme, PowerPlay Strategies Inc, and Youth Entrepreneurship programme, Vancity is truly cultivating dreams.

Generation 'Y entrepreneurs

Young entrepreneurs with sound business ideas and business acumen are getting a helping hand through an innovative new program in B.C.

Canadian Youth Business Foundation (CYBF), a non-profit national organization, is the national leader in providing full service support to tomorrow's business leaders to start and grow successful businesses. VanCity has recently partnered with CYBF to provide loans to youth referred by CYBF of up to $15,000 to start their business.

Modeled after the Prince's Youth Business Trust in the UK, the CYBF provides resources, mentoring, and loans to youth aged 18-34. One of the key successes to the program is a comprehensive mentoring program designed to support young entrepreneurs at various stages of business development. Volunteer mentors, often with years of business expertise, make a long-term commitment to meet regularly to provide advice and support. Youth learn skills such as marketing and sales.

Until now, CYBF has been using its own investment capital to provide loans to participants. With backing from Western Economic Diversification, VanCity will now be providing loan capital to CYBF-referred youth businesses in order to free up CYBF's resources for other programs. ■

To find out more or to apply for youth loans, contact CYBF directly at www.cybf.ca or call 604 412-7642.

ADVERTISEMENT FOR THE YOUTH PROGRAMME

YOUTH CO-OPERATIVISTS ATTENDING A COUNCIL MEETING

4

ARGENTINIAN
Co-operatives Association (ACA)

Central Agrarian Co-operativist
YOUTH COUNCIL

Argentina

Date of Incorporation: November 1st, 1944

Membership: The Council is made up of 48 co-operativist agrarian youth groups organized in ten Regional Youth Advising Commissions. There are approximately 2,000 young people, all engaged in rural activities, associated with these local organisations.

Activity: The Council encourages improved technical production of agricultural goods and is involved in management training for projects conceived by the young people themselves.

Organisational Form: Association

Service Area: The Council is active in the provinces of Buenos Aires, Córdoba, Santa Fe, Río Negro, La Pampa, Entre Ríos, Misiones and Corrientes.

Antecedents / Context

The Agrarian Co-operativist Youth was organized in 1944 in response to challenges being faced by the agrarian co-operative movement. Today, it is particularly interested in moving beyond its original goals to help the new generations to develop all kinds of co-operative endeavour. Through working within the ACA, agrarian youth contribute by ensuring the survival of co-operatives and the better understanding of co-operativism.

Vision/Intention/Goals

The slogan: "To educate humanity and to cultivate the earth" summarises the Agrarian Co-operativist Youth's basic objective.

The co-op's mission is to train co-operative people who can work as farming entrepreneurs able to manage their operations effectively and to participate in the decision making of their co-operative as truly responsible members. We encourage co-operative people to embrace attitudes of service in their different communities, working together to respond to their concerns and needs through social, technical, educational, and cultural activities carried out in accordance with co-operative doctrine.

Goals

- To contribute to the growth of co-operative culture in all environments and particularly in rural areas.
- To organize, co-ordinate, and disseminate the agrarian youth movement associated with the co-operatives that make up the ACA.

THE COUNCIL'S BOARD OF DIRECTORS

- To contribute to a wider understanding of the basic economic and social issues of the Nation and a greater appreciation of the influence of the farming economy.
- To encourage the development of co-operativism in all its forms and to disseminate its doctrines.
- To maintain permanent cultural relationships with all youth members and to create links with similar entities in Argentina and around the world.
- To collaborate with various institutions in encouraging better farming production and in disseminating knowledge gained from research, science, and technological advances.
- To help young farmers gain the technical training they need, and
- To help provide university training in the rural environment.

Organisational Structure / Model Used

The organisation operates on three levels, starting with local youth groups in each primary co-operative joined to the ACA. The core organisation is the Central Youth Council. Between those two levels there is the "Regional Youth Advisory Commission" (CARJ) concerned with regional co-ordination and divided into geographical zones as predetermined by the ACA structure. The decision making process is dynamic and participatory in nature. With issues requiring consensus, the Central Council's proposals are passed on to the CARJ. Grass roots youth in each zone are consulted individually and their input is then passed back to the Central Council. Daily issues are decided by the Central Council delegates.

The Council's Board of Directors provides direction in the development of policies regarding our participation in co-operative and rural activities. It is made up of 19 members elected from the Central Youth Council, which is made up of two representatives from each zone. Within the Board, the executive committee leads the discussions, prepares proposals, develops projects, and works on issues of urgency or priority. None of the members of the executive committee or the permanent delegates of the Council is paid. There is no subscribing to shares, since the Central Agrarian Youth Council, as a member of the ACA, does not have legal status.

Links with the Community / Networks / Scope

Youth groups, generally acting in towns of less than 20,000 inhabitants, establish broad links with the community. For many young people in the country the greatest value of participating in the movement consists of being able to count on new opportunities for sharing attitudes and life experiences with their equals, discussing production problems and planning joint development projects.

Future Plans

The short-term goals are to consolidate the organisational structure and to work on meeting concrete needs. If we address the big issues of rural life, then our growth will be assured.

In the long term, we plan collaborate with the ACA and ultimately consolidate our activities in order to have a strong overall structure for management and technical/practical training. Co-operative action needs to be readdressed from the ground up, starting with the principles of solidarity and encouraging young people as agents of local change. It is paramount to overcome the mistrust many youth feel towards the co-operative structure and the weight of an older leadership. The co-op is determined to contest the economic and social instability of the country, the kind of instability that is driving many young people out of rural areas.

Present Issues

- Developing growth strategies for education, technology, and development through embracing the themes of "Co-operative – Families – Society".
- Advancing new training and educational programmes that will respond to the needs of rural youth.

Advice

Young people should avoid distorting the co-operatives' activities and should follow the essential principles of co-operative doctrine. Co-operatives have a lot of work yet to do and must take steps to improve their performance. It is important to celebrate the accomplishments of the past, embrace co-operative ideals, and create very clear guidelines for the future.

Coast Capital Savings Credit Union, Canada

As one of Canada's 50 Best Managed Companies, Coast Capital Savings offers a great opportunity for grade 11 and 12 high school students in Richmond, Surrey and on Vancouver Island to get a jump start on life with real-world experience both on the job and in the community. Hired by the credit union to be part of The Coast Community Youth Team, the students work for a one-year term at community events and as Customer Service Representatives at a Coast Capital Savings branch, gaining valuable leadership, interpersonal and job-related skills.

COAST CAPITAL
SAVINGS
Credit Union

Canada

"The business aspect of the program is important because the students learn how to work in a professional environment," said Debi Dempsey. "After a year with this

2004-2005 RICHMOND COAST COMMUNITY YOUTH TEAM

program, the students have skills that many of their peers haven't had the opportunity to develop."

Coast Capital Savings is Canada's second largest credit union. It has 44 branches across the Lower Mainland, Fraser Valley and Vancouver Island of British Columbia. It was the recipient of the 2004 *Imagine Award* for being the best corporate citizen in Canada's financial services industry.

"Applying for the program was one of the best decisions of my life," said Rob Davies, a former member of the Coast Community Youth Team. "This experience has made an incredible impact on my life both personally and professionally. My time as a Coast Community Youth Team member has given me the confidence and skills I need to succeed."

Jemina Tolentino knows just what Rob is talking about. One of six Richmond students hired for the 2003/2004 Coast Community Youth Team, Jemina says the program also helped her to gain self-confidence and develop new skills.

"As part of the Coast Community Youth Team, I had the opportunity to become more involved in my community and to learn more about the financial services industry," she said. "It's a big commitment, but it's a great job."

Like Rob, Jemina chose to continue working for Coast Capital Savings after her one-year term ended.

2004-2005 RICHMOND AND SURREY
COAST COMMUNITY YOUTH TEAMS

"More than 165 students have gone through this program since 1993," said Debi Dempsey, Community Relations Manager at Coast Capital Savings. "75 per cent of the students who join the Coast Community Youth Team continue to work for us after their term ends."

Each year, Coast Capital Savings recruits 12 students on the Island, six in Richmond and six in Surrey for the program. These students are given countless hours of community relations training, which helps to prepare them for the more than 90 family-oriented events and parades that the Team attends across Vancouver Island, the Lower Mainland and the Fraser Valley every year.

ISLAND COAST COMMUNITY YOUTH TEAM MEMBERS WITH THE CREDIT UNION'S MASCOT, WALLY THE WHALE.

The primary role of the students at these events is to interact with children through face painting, administering a child ID program and performing as the credit union's mascot, Wally the Whale.

During their one-year term, the students are also required to complete a volunteer project. The 40 hours of volunteer time can be applied towards their graduation requirements.

The Island Coast Community Youth Team has participated in a cleanup of the Gorge Waterway in Victoria for a number of years. With the help of 100 volunteers, the Team pulled over two tonnes of waste from the Gorge Waterway in 2004, including lawn chairs, car parts and shopping carts.

THE ISLAND COAST COMMUNITY YOUTH TEAM
ORGANISED THE GORGE WATERWAY CLEANUP IN 2004

The Team wrote a grant application to the city, canvassed local businesses for prizes, contacted past volunteers and organized the set up and clean up for the event.

For their volunteer project, the 2004/2005 Richmond Coast Community Youth Team chose to help landscape an undeveloped area for use as a community garden and park.

TEAM MEMBERS REMOVING A SHOPPING
CART FROM THE WATERWAY

CELEBRATING THE REMOVAL OF TWO TONNES
OF WASTE FROM THE WATERWAY

"It felt great to give something back to the community and when I visit in the future, I'll know that I helped make that park possible," said Martin Hui, a member of the 2004/2005 Richmond Coast Community Youth Team.

When the Team is not out at community events, the students work in the branches as Customer Service Representatives.

The Youth Advisory Committee was developed in 1993 by Pacific Coast Savings as a way for the credit union to get involved in local community events while providing a unique job opportunity to youth on Vancouver Island.

When Pacific Coast Savings became Coast Capital Savings in 2000, the program was expanded to include Richmond and Surrey and renamed The Coast Community Youth Team.

"The program has been a tremendous success," said Debi Dempsey, Community Relations Manager, Coast Capital Savings. "It is truly a delight to mentor these young people and watch them grow and develop."

For more information on the Coast Community Youth Team, visit http://www.coastcapitalsavings.com.

YOUTH REINVENTING CO-OPERATIVES

6

Federation of
YOUNG
CO-OPERATORS

Argentina

Date of Incorporation: July 1999

Membership: The Federation of Co-operativist Youth encompasses approximately 1000 young people from ages 14 to 35.

Youth Centre Activities

At the time of its establishment, the Federation of Co-operativist Youth had the sole objective of educating and training young people in co-operative matters. Since then, it has incorporated productive endeavours.

Some of the activities currently undertaken by the Co-operativist Youth Centres are:

Productive Projects:

- Poultry Farms
- Grain Plantations
- Communal Market Gardens (Horticulture)

- Tobacco Plantations
- Small Plastic Bags Manufacturing
- Canvas Shoes (Espadrilles) Manufacturing
- Forest Nursery
- Beekeeping
- Regional Wood Craftwork Manufacturing
- Co-operative Bakery

Training and Vocational Activities:

- Co-operative Education
- Project Evaluation Courses
- Co-operative Management Courses
- Seminars on School Co-operatives
- Computer Courses
- Tour Guide Training
- Communal School Library Project

Social and Dissemination Activities:

- Organisation of Inter-School Olympics
- Notes, Reports, and Dissemination of the Co-operative Youth Movement
- Awarding of Scholarships
- Co-operative Newspaper
- Organisation of Co-operative Youth Camps
- Radio Programme on Co-operative Interests

Antecedents / Context

Starting in 1998, Argentina's Northeast Region went through the worst socio-economic crisis in its history. Corrientes was particularly affected because of its large farm production base and scarce population. The economic crisis offered an uncertain future, especially for the young people.

Some groups of young people started to organize themselves, in the process emphasizing such values as solidarity, co-operation, *asociativismo*, and ethics.

Objectives

- Encouraging, promoting, and developing Youth Centres
- Representing the Youth Centres in Public and Private Organisations

- Organising and participating in courses, seminars, and similar activities
- Creating a space for exchanging co-operative experiences
- Supporting programmes and activities encouraging the young people's complete fulfillment within the co-operative environment
- Promoting cultural exchange programmes among youth in the region
- Encouraging the development of co-operative youth ventures for production and/or service

Organisation's Beginnings

The initiative arose with a group of students who set out to work together with young people associated with the co-operative movement in the Province of Corrientes. They organised themselves first into Youth Centres and then into the Federation of Co-operativist Youths.

They encountered some difficulties in the early period. One problem was that some parents believed it would be better for the young people to remain focused on their work rather than on attending training activities. Another problem was that some political activists tried to use the co-operative to build support during elections.

> Some groups of young people started to organize themselves, in the process emphasizing such values as solidarity, co-operation, asociativismo, and ethics.

Organisational Structure

There are ten Youth Centres attached to the Federation, which is run by a Board of Directors. The Federation's board is made up of six permanent members (president, vice-president, secretary, pro-secretary, treasurer, and pro-treasurer), one permanent trustee and one substitute. It is operated under two-year mandates that are reviewed annually. In addition, two representatives from each of the Youth Centres can participate at Board meetings, having the right to both speak and vote.

Members from the Centres can use the Federation's services, actively participate in its assemblies, run for the Board of Directors, participate in the elections, and propose initiatives for consideration by the Board and the Assemblies. They also have free access to the information that the Federation provides.

The organization is funded by contributions made by the members (fifty pesos per year) and through donations received from associates and other public or private institutions.

Within the Federation, an authority, called Department of Youth, is in charge of managing, organising, and supervising the activities taking place. It also reviews suggested projects from the various Youth Centres, finding financial resources and supporting project development.

This Department has three working areas: institutional relationships, internal development, and management development. Administratively, it is divided into four branches: management, accounting, education, and productive projects.

Links to the Community / Networks

The young people making up the Educational Committee visit provinces in the whole country in order to educate and train young co-operativist leaders. Members of the Committee work together with the National Institute of Association and Social Economy, the Federation of Co-operatives of Corrientes, and the Provincial Headquarters of Co-operatives, as well as other provincial organisations of education, national and provincial authorities supporting small producers, and national universities.

> "The organization is funded by contributions made by the members (fifty pesos per year) and through donations received from associates and other public or private institutions."

Federation members can also attend the meetings of the Board of Directors to address issues that affect rural co-operatives at the national level, as well as those of importance to urban co-operatives.

Lessons Learned

One of the most important lessons learned is that a good provincial co-operativist leader needs to be able to go out and find out what is happening in the country. He or she should not be satisfied to remain seated behind a desk.

It is also important to have strong associations with the provincial co-operative movement. Young people learn from what adults have done well and not so well. Having a range of ages involved helps to bring continuity to already developed tasks and allows generational succession to happen under more experienced leadership.

Finally, gathering into local youth centres has enabled youth to develop an effective process of social and cultural integration, which allows them to respond to the need for personal advancement as well as for community growth. A youth project run by youth can find solutions to the various issues emerging within the working, social, educational, and productive environments in which they live.

We can also be pleased as we measure success in quantitative terms and can see how a great number of young people have benefited from the Federation's activities. Furthermore, we can also measure success qualitatively as we review the development of solid productive projects, dissemination activities, and institutional participation.

MEMBERS OF A FARMING & RANCHING CO-OP –
THE GUILLERMO LEHMANN CO-OPERATIVE

Farming & Ranching Youth
for CO-OPERATIVE
DEVELOPMENT

Argentina

Date of Incorporation: August 1999

Membership: Fifty-eight members aged fifteen to thirty-five years, 33% women, 67 % men.

Activity: The youth group is dedicated to training young people so that they can more easily integrate into farming and ranching activities.

Organisational Form: The co-op is not a legal entity but a statute establishes our operating regulations and defines how our officials will be elected.

Service Area: Departments of Las Colonias, Castellanos and La Capital, located in the centre of the Province of Santa Fe.

Antecedents / Context

The association arose within the Guillermo Lehmann Farming and Ranching Co-operative Ltd. It began from a desire to bring young people closer to the co-operative so that they would participate in its activities and be ready to succeed as leaders of it, when the time comes. The initial group was formed by 15 young farm and ranch producers and the children of farm and ranch producers. They all lived in or near a small town of 5,000 inhabitants in the Province of Santa Fe, Argentina; they had not had access to higher education.

They started by observing the experiences of some other co-operatives. They conducted an opinion poll among young people to see what they wanted and then hired a professional advisor to help them form a youth group.

Our first economic resources came from the Guillermo Lehmann Co-operative and from the co-operative education and training fund. We also received subsidies from the Management of the Province's Co-operatives, from other co-operatives, and from the local community and private ventures.

Obstacles

One of the first obstacles was that the young people initially had strong feelings of individualism. They had to work hard before they were able to think and act as a group.

The main current difficulties have been: (a) stimulating interest among young people so that the co-op can be incorporated and (b) the difficulty heads of farming and ranching ventures have in finding the time to be involved in co-op activities.

Vision / Mission / Goals

Our vision is to be a rural co-operative entity helping to shape the development of youth socially and morally, while providing them with the technical training needed to continue in the co-operative context and also achieve a better quality of life. Our mission is to provide young rural co-operaters with the tools they require to satisfy their needs, farm more effectively, and apply the co-operative doctrine more completely.

Since we have the support of a farming and ranching co-operative, we explored the co-operative form carefully and chose it because of its goodness and appropriateness and its capacities to meet the idiosyncrasies of the area. Thanks to its qualities as a democratic, participatory, and autonomous organisation, the co-operative model conforms to the needs and aspirations of youth. It also offers them opportunities to receive training and to integrate socially.

Organisational Structure

The structure resembles that of the Guillermo Lehmann Co-operative. The highest authority is the assembly of members, which meets at least once a year. A board of directors, consisting of nine permanent and three substitute members, is responsible for the co-operative's management. There is also an Executive Committee, which includes a president, a vice-president, a treasurer, a secretary, and a permanent and a substitute trustee. The different tasks are organised into work commissions.

The professional advisor, who graduated in co-operative studies, co-ordinates the activities and manages the organisation and is the only person to receive a salary (which is paid by the Guillermo Lehmann Co-operative). The members of the Executive Committee only receive reimbursement for expenses when participating in an activity that draws them away from their work

Although the co-operative's by-laws require members to pay an entry fee in order to join the group, this requirement has not been enforced.

Members who are not part of the board participate through open meetings and in member assemblies in which they have speaking and voting rights. In our meetings, the priority is to search for consensus and vote only when there are differences in opinions or in proposals.

MEMBERS IN A MEETING

Links to the Community/Network/Scope

The young people are linked to multiple organisations within the community to which they belong, including educational entities, co-operatives, private ventures, and other institutions of the Province of Santa Fe. They are also involved in the Regional Network of Co-operativist Farming and Ranching Youth and the Network of Rural Co-operativist Youth of the South Cone. These activities have helped young people to open their minds and to undertake more ambitious activities within the region.

Achievement

By being involved in the co-operative, some young people have been appointed or hired to jobs in co-operatives, other institutions, and private ventures in the area. They have made important social contacts and they have been able to travel to neighbouring countries.

The success of the Co-op is measured by observing that those who have gone through the youth centre are now leaders in their community and successful entrepreneurs in their farming and ranching operations; they know about and defend the co-operative system. Some of them have already joined the board of directors of the co-operative that sponsored them; others have been able to secure a job working in the farming and ranching industries.

Future Plans

In the short term, the co-op's goal is to continue co-operative training programmes and to attract more youth from neighbouring towns to join our group.

In the longer term, the co-op will venture into productive activities, offering services to the community and making the organisation self-sufficient; remaining dependent upon the Guillermo Lehmann Co-operative for funding is not satisfactory.

Learned Lessons

Teamwork depends on a person's individual skills, and we believe it is important to value the abilities of young people. Young people are able to undertake complex and risky activities. By encouraging young people to undertake a variety of tasks, they will be rewarded by what they do and they will grow as individuals.

Advice

Governments should support and encourage this type of organisation, since it can be very beneficial for young people trying to build their futures. Governments should consider forming strategic alliances with youth organisations to undertake such activities as the provision of public services and the construction of housing by co-operatives.

Co-operatives should encourage the creation of youth groups so that they will be able to count on generational succession and continuity into the future.

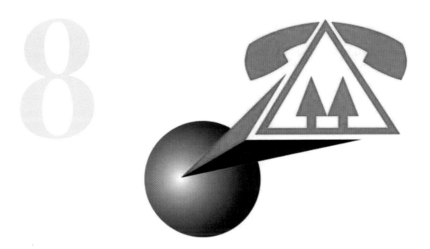

Suardi's
Telephone and Public Services Limited
CO-OPERATIVIST YOUTH CENTRE

Argentina

Date of Incorporation: The Centre was officially formed in January 2004.

Membership: We have 18 members.

Area of Service: Suardi, town of San Cristobal, Province of Santa Fe. The town has 6,229 inhabitants, 79% urban.

Activities:

We are primarily concerned with disseminating the co-operative's services. We develop training programmes and workshops for the young people in the region. We hold meetings and activities with different institutions in the area to make people aware of the main issues that concern us and to help plan our activities in the short and longer term. We organize clothing and food collections for distribution among the most needy in the community. We organize regional meetings for co-operativist youth.

Organisational Form:

We are an association without legal registration because we are organized within the Suardi's Telephone and Public Services Co-operative Limited. We co-ordinate our activities with other co-operative centres and youth groups belonging to the co-operative telephone movement of the Federation of Telecommunications Co-operatives Limited – FECOTEL Ltda.

Identified Needs:

- Lack of adult interest in co-operative projects and ventures carried out by the young people
- Shortage of spaces in which to undertake the co-operatives' activities
- Lack of work options in the community

Antecedents/Context:

Suardi's Telephone and Public Services Co-operative Limited was founded in 1958 as an electrical co-operative. In 1964 it started to provide urban and rural telephone services and installed 1,540 lines. It functioned until 1978, when the generation and distribution of electric energy passed into the hands of the Provincial State. Presently, it offers other types of services, such as: free Internet for schools, libraries, and other institutions, and assistance in health facilities and in the hotel business industry.

In the year 2000 the co-operative called a meeting with the town's young people to discuss how they could be integrated within the field of co-operative work. In 2004 the Centre was launched as a way to associate several co-operative activities with the development of projects for the community.

Vision:

- Consolidate youth action to develop future leadership for the community
- Actively participate in the co-operative movement at local, regional, and national levels

Mission:

- Encourage youth participation in co-operatives
- Organize events that will contribute to local development
- Raise awareness of, and care for, environmental issues
- Promote co-operative training
- Instil the co-operativist spirit and encourage solidarity

Organisational Structure:

A Board of Directors made up by ten permanent members and four substitutes provides leadership for the Centre.

Links with the Community:

Our programme builds on the links traditionally held by the telephone co-operative with institutions in the area, especially in education, in both rural and urban districts. Our co-operative interests facilitate relationships with the traditional co-operatives in the farming and ranching sector.

Resources:

Since our work is associated with co-operative activity, we can draw on resources provided by the Co-operative Education and Training Fund, implemented by the Law of Co-operatives.

Future Plans:

- Develop and promote activities oriented toward youth, especially those encouraging work within our area.
- Concentrate on our training activities.
- Help expand and improve green spaces in the Suardi community.

Present Issues:

- Improve employment opportunities for young people in rural and urban areas.
- Strengthen training activities for youth oriented toward communal promotion and participation.
- Improve the capacity of young people to make decisions and communicate effectively.
- Encourage new members to participate in the Centre's activities.

Messages:

- Help mobilize youth who now are indifferent to the problems of the community.
- Demonstrate with action that change is possible.
- Show those who believe problems are insolvable that, through solidarity much can be accomplished.
- Discover the true role of the young people in the community and communicate that to the adults.
- Learn to work in teams in order to reach objectives, goals, and ends among youth and adults, thereby bridging generational differences.

CO-OPERATIVE SCHOOL PIONEERS

YOUTH AND STAFF POSING FOR PHOTO:
SWIFT CURRENT CO-OP SCHOOL 1948

Michelle Korven is the Program Officer with the Saskatchewan Co-operative Association and Manages the Saskatchewan Co-operative Youth Program. Michelle graduated from the University of Saskatchewan in 2002. Michelle was born and raised on the Saskatchewan prairies in the small town of Cabri. Michelle grew up on the land that her great-grandfather homesteaded in the early 1900's, and where her parents continue to farm. She is a strong supporter of the co-operative movement and is dedicated to helping youth explore their potential and develop the skills that will help them to succeed as community conscious citizens.

Michelle Korven
Canada

9

The Saskatchewan
YOUTH
PROGRAMME

Michelle Korven

In the early 1900s co-operatives were the saving grace for many Saskatchewan farmers and their families on the Canadian prairies. The co-operative movement grew steadily in Saskatchewan for many years, and the people of Saskatchewan attributed much of their survival and success, often amid natural disasters, depressions and low prices, to the co-operative way of working together. They developed co-operatives to market their grains, dairy and poultry production. They created co-operative stores to meet their consumer needs, credit unions to provide financial services, curling rinks for winter amusements, community groups to fund medical services, and bull rings to improve the quality of their herds.

As early as the 1920s, the pioneers of the co-op movement were concerned that the movement might not continue in Saskatchewan if it did not actively educate youth on the co-op model and its benefits. They wanted to ensure that Saskatchewan youth understood the significant role co-operatives had played in making survival possible for many rural people on the Prairies. They decided to start educating Saskatchewan youth on why co-operatives are so important and that co-operation is a way of life that really works.

> As most people living on the Prairies during the 30's were accustomed to co-operating as a way of survival, they responded to the destitution of the Great Depression by working together to help themselves.

Originally named, "Co-op Schools," the first one-day seminar was held in 1928 and was organized for anyone who wished to become familiar with co-operative principles, particularly young adults. Thirty-eight Co-op Schools were held that year and they drew a positive response from both those in charge and those in attendance. The popularity of the Co-op Schools necessitated growth. By 1929, 127 one-day seminars were being held in different locations across Saskatchewan. The majority of attendees were farmers and committeemen from the Saskatchewan Wheat Pool, the main grain-marketing co-operative in the province. While most of those attending were older, many were younger – in their twenties and early thirties. The Co-op Schools attracted great interest and would have continued after 1929, but, when the stock market crashed and the Great Depression swept over the Prairies, there were not enough financial resources to keep the Co-op Schools going. There is no recorded Co-op School activity between 1930 and 1937.

As most people living on the Prairies during the 30's were accustomed to co-operating as a way of survival, they responded to the destitution of the Great Depression by working together to help themselves. The Depression stimulated the creation of many new kinds of co-operatives all over Saskatchewan. As these new co-operatives were organized and grew, it became apparent that more specialized co-operative training was needed.

In response to this increased need, the first weeklong Co-op School seminar was held at the University of Saskatchewan in June 1937. This seminar had a broader scope in subjects than the previous one-day events. The participants received intensive and specialized training in the areas of co-operative marketing and in the operation of the co-operative business model. These longer seminars were a huge success and continued in a similar fashion through World War II and into the 1960s.

> Co-op Schools had a major role in fostering the development of the Co-operative College of Canada (later merged with the Co-operative Union of Canada to become the Canadian Co-operative Association).

By that time, though, a new attitude toward education and learning techniques was beginning to emerge. There was considerable demand for the use of more varied teaching techniques, including the use of more visual aids and increased student participation. In response to the demand, Co-op School session leaders started moving away from lecture techniques and towards group discussions aimed at encouraging an increased understanding among participants. The Co-op Schools were taking on new objectives, including individual and group development. There was also a change in the way that discipline was achieved in the Schools. The students, who had once been under fairly firm discipline applied by the instructors, were given more freedom and responsibility for their actions. Decision-making became a more democratic process involving both Co-op School participants and staff.

As the Co-op Schools grew in size and popularity, it was evident that there was a need to formalize the weeklong seminars and ensure high quality, consistent co-operative education. In that regard, Co-op Schools had a major role in fostering the development of the Co-operative College of Canada (later merged with the Co-operative Union of Canada to become the Canadian Co-operative Association). Co-op Schools became the responsibility of the College, and the seminars were held in Saskatoon at its facilities.

During the 1960s the focus of co-operative education moved even more towards the younger generation. In 1966 the first Junior Co-op School was held for youth between the ages of thirteen and fifteen. Before this time, the people attending the Co-op Schools had been mainly in their late teens and twenties.

By 1970, it was felt that even the term "Co-op School" was a bit misleading because lessons on co-operatives were no longer the only concern. Living together in a social and working environment

BOYS SWIMMING CLASS AT CO-OP SCHOOL, SWIFT CURRENT, SASKATCHEWAN, 1956

YOUTH IN LARGE CIRCLE AT PRINCE ALBERT CO-OP SCHOOL, JULY 9, 1947

was gaining more importance. A new name, The Saskatchewan Co-operative Youth Programme, was formally adopted in 1970.

The Saskatchewan Co-operative Youth Programme has changed significantly over the past 76 years. The original intent, however, "to grow with the co-operative sector and educate people on the benefits of co-operatives", is still a part of today's programme. Today, the aim of the Saskatchewan Co-operative Youth Programme (SCYP) is to contribute to the personal development of youth and encourage their active involvement in community and co-operative organisations. Each summer, during the months of July and August, seven seminars are offered to Saskatchewan teens, between the ages of fourteen and eighteen. The seminars are held in a camp-like setting and their focus is on fun, learning, and personal growth.

> The Saskatchewan Co-operative Youth Programme has changed significantly over the past 76 years. The original intent, however, "to grow with the co-operative sector and educate people on the benefits of co-operatives", is still a part of today's programme.

SCYP seminars are an opportunity for Saskatchewan youth to gain important life skills, such as leadership, communication, co-operative behaviour, public speaking, teamwork and self-esteem. The seminars instil responsibility, as participants are responsible for organizing a co-operative to plan and run the week, and for chores such as cooking and cleaning. This gives the participants a sense of ownership of the seminar and helps everyone to bond with everyone else, developing rewarding and lasting relationships.

SASKATCHEWAN CO-OPERATIVE YOUTH
PROGRAMME PARTICIPANTS, 2004

The Saskatchewan Co-operative Youth Programme has evolved into a three-year progressive programme. Each five or six day seminar that participants attend builds on what they have learned at previous seminars. Each level has curriculum that staff uses to ensure quality, consistent education. Although the Youth Programme is highly educational, it bears little resemblance to the more traditional methods of teaching. Skill development takes place through interactive, experiential learning. The participants work together to do activities and solve challenges – so the learning is always fun and hands-on. However, the Youth Programme seminars are not all about the lessons – a significant portion of the week is spent doing the usual fun camp activities, like canoeing, swimming, campfires, volleyball and other games.

> The SCYP seminars are staffed by employees and elected officials from the co-operative sector, as well as programme alumni who volunteer their time.

The SCYP seminars are staffed by employees and elected officials from the co-operative sector, as well as programme alumni who volunteer their time. Staff responsibilities include: planning the seminar, developing and leading sessions, participating in sessions, organizing social and recreational events, supervising participants, being involved in cooking and clean-up, and participating in daily staff meetings. Staffing a Youth Seminar is a great opportunity for staff to help make a difference in the lives of young people; to meet and work with other co-operative sector employees; to polish presentation and facilitation skills; and to learn all kinds of things about co-operatives and the co-operative way of working together. Many staff members return

SCYP SEMINARS INCLUDE MANY FUN ACTIVITIES LIKE CANOEING

year after year because of their enjoyment of the seminars and the personal growth they experience.

Attending a Co-operative Youth Programme seminar opens up a world of opportunities for Saskatchewan youth. It has been a significant way in which young people have been able to prepare themselves for the work place. Some previous participants have gone on to become Junior Staff or summer students in the Youth Programme office. Some have participated in overseas exchanges or gained employment in Saskatchewan co-operatives as a result of their participation in the programme. Attendance at an SCYP seminar is highly regarded on a résumé because it tells future employers that the youth have learned about co-operatives, that they are serious about learning new skills, and that they have polished their communication and leadership abilities.

The Saskatchewan Co-operative Youth Programme is the single largest programme managed by the Saskatchewan Co-operative Association (SCA). The members of the SCA are: Saskatchewan Wheat Pool, Credit Union Central of Saskatchewan, Federated Co-operatives Limited, The Co-operators, Concentra Financial Services Association, The CUMIS Group, Community Health Co-operative Federation, Saskatchewan Federation of Production Co-operatives, Co-operative Housing Federation of Canada, Access Communications Co-operative, and the Canadian Worker Co-operative Federation. Each participant who attends a seminar pays a registration fee. In addition, a local co-operative pays a sponsorship fee. The seminars are held at Hannin Creek

Camp, Candle Lake, northeast of Prince Albert, and chartered bus transportation is provided from Saskatoon up to the seminar site.

The Saskatchewan Co-operative Youth Programme has been successful for more than 75 years. It has been estimated that more than 41,948 Saskatchewan-based young adults have attended a Co-op School or a Co-operative Youth Seminar. This is an unmistakable sign that the programme has truly touched the lives of Saskatchewan people. Although the programme has changed significantly throughout its history, the focus and intention behind the programme has only strengthened. The uniqueness of the programme stems from its ability to provide a co-operative, participatory learning experience for young people, co-op staff and volunteers within a positive, enjoyable environment.

Objectives of the Saskatchewan Co-operative Youth Programme

- To develop communication, leadership and group participation skills in young people;
- To develop young people who demonstrate co-operative values;
- To develop community responsibility and encourage young people to support and become involved in their communities using co-operative approaches;
- To develop young people who recognize and understand co-operatives including their social and economic benefits;
- To promote active involvement in co-operatives in young people; and
- To provide sponsoring organisations with information relative to the expectations and needs of young people.

SCYP PARTICIPANTS PLAYING VOLLEYBALL

The Saskatchewan Co-operative Youth Programme Statement of Values

Respect

The SCYP has a fundamental respect for people. We honour the uniqueness of the individual and the value of groups. Respect fosters openness and authentic self-expression which, in turn, builds trust. We enhance this trusting atmosphere through sharing, listening and respecting confidentiality.

Co-operation

The SCYP values co-operation and democratic practices. We value the input of each individual, and through teamwork, we effectively achieve our goals. Through group decision-making and communication we generate a spirit of co-operation and a sense of community.

Equality

The SCYP respects the equality of all people. We believe in social responsibility, justice and economic empowerment through co-operatives. We welcome a diversity of beliefs, cultures and values in our programme. We act to include this diversity.

Development

The SCYP values the growth and development of people and their co-operatives. We contribute to personal growth through education, participation and skill development that in turn benefits co-operatives. Our programmes serve as an information link between youth and co-operatives in Saskatchewan.

Interdependence

The SCYP believes in the interdependence of people. We build a social bond between individuals through understanding, consideration and interaction. We act with a responsibility to care for others.

Amanda Sharp, United Kingdom

Amanda Sharp is the Projects Co-ordinator at the Co-operative College, Manchester, the United Kingdom.

10
CHAIN

Building Co-operative Futures

Amanda Sharp

Base: Manchester, England

Started: November 2003

This network started off with just two people, Simon Plunkett, Member Services Officer at the Co-operative Group and Amanda Sharp, Projects Co-ordinator at the Co-operative College. It now has a steering group of seven with representation from different areas of co-operative business, and it has over 250 members registered on its database.

How did we do it?

In November 2003, the Co-operative Group (the largest consumer co-operative society in the UK with an annual turnover of more than £8 billion), and more specifically the Group's Values and Principles Committee, decided they would like to support and encourage youth activities amongst their employees in the Manchester hub base. This consisted of about 8,000 people (although not all were youth) who worked with The Co-operative Group, Co-operatives UK, Co-operative Financial Services and the Co-operative College. We were given a period of six months to see what we could achieve with a budget of £4000.

The aims of the network were to expand employee membership amongst the younger staff members (eighteen to thirty-five years old); to educate others on the different areas of co-operative business, the co-operative movement in the UK and wider world; to link with the Co-operative Group's Northern regional membership office; and to provide a social environment in which people could build friendships and working relationships.

The Co-operative Group is a national society and has regional offices throughout the UK. Whenever possible, Chain tries to link up with any activities that the Northern membership team carries out, especially

HAVING FUN AND PAINTING CO-OPERATIVELY

YOUTH REINVENTING CO-OPERATIVES

**COMMUNITY PROJECT – MURAL PAINTING
AT A LOCAL COMMUNITY CENTRE**

their events held specifically for young people, though the team is very new and has only just started running events. In October 2004, we held our first weekend event in Rochdale, the birthplace of the British Co-operative Movement.

With all of our objectives in mind, we began to think about what should be done first. The priority was to appoint a steering group, as we realised it was a huge task trying to engage so many people in the complex. Therefore, from contacts we already had and recommendations from peers and managers, we approached two people from the retail side of the business – Rachel Burlton and Kerry Silke. They were both enthusiastic and keen to be involved. Soon after this, we were approached by Sarah France from the Learning Centre – a centre that runs courses for employees of the Co-operative Group, from sign language to self-defence.

 We liked the idea of linking rings representing the different areas of business, and felt it illustrated that we were one link in the Chain of the co-operative movement.

Sarah was enthusiastic about the project. As she later put it:

> I believe that young people have a lot to give and sometimes they are under estimated and misunderstood by others within the community and the workplace. Chain gives young people at the Co-operative Head Office in Manchester a voice.

Our next priority was to establish a name that was representative of the entire complex. We discussed the different names we could have and what those names would represent, and finally we chose Chain. We liked the idea of linking rings representing the different areas of business, and felt it illustrated that we were one link in the Chain of the co-operative movement. For the logo we deliberately chose the ring styles and colours used for the Olympic Games, as we saw this as a symbol of unification. The design of the logo and headed paper was carried out by a contact from Co-op Retail

HALLOWEEN "FRIGHT NIGHT" ORGANISERS

at a reduced rate. This is just one example of the support we've received from the co-operative movement since starting the project.

We worked towards our first event, which was the launch of the network in February 2004. We invited Martin Beaumont, Chief Executive of the Co-operative Group, and Bob Burlton, Chair Designate of the Co-operative Group and chief executive of Oxford, Swindon and Gloucester Co-operative Society, to speak at the event about why the network is a good idea, what they hoped the outcomes would be, and the importance for the Co-operative Group in the future. This event was an important one so we put a lot of time and effort into it. It paid off. The event was well attended and many of the original attendees remain our most active members.

As news about Chain spread, more events were planned and we realised we needed more help. From the launch event, two people came forward showing interest in Chain and were later asked to join the steering group. They were Alan Hale and Paul Donlan from Co-operative Financial Services. Unfortunately, due to other commitments, Paul had to leave the group some six months later.

With a steering group of six, we felt we had real representation from all areas of the complex and we started to set up a timetable of events.

Some of those events are listed below:

March 04 – Marketing our Co-operative Advantage seminar with Tom Webb

May 04 – Co-operative Congress – an opportunity to see behind the scenes and attend the workshops

June 04 – Co-operative Action – A Kick Start for Co-operation!

August 04 – Community Project – painting a mural on the sports hall wall of a local community centre.

Sept 04 – *Ghouls, Ghosts and Legends of the Co-operative Movement* – A walking tour of Manchester City Centre, taking in Co-op History over the last 150 years.

October 04 – Halloween "Fright Night" Party for children at a local community centre

We also funded two people to attend international events: the second annual Building Co-operative Futures conference in Calgary, Canada, in May 2004, and the International Co-operative Alliance's European Assembly in Warsaw, Poland, in September 2004.

Terry Clennell was the Chain representative who attended the ICA youth seminar in Poland. He says,

> I see Chain as a multipurpose organisation, being a means of promoting the values that youth can bring to the co-op, acting as a platform to network and encouraging the development of youth throughout the business; and a forum to enlighten members about co-operative values and

A GHASTLY GHOUL OF FRIGHT NIGHT

principles. It goes without saying that I believe it has to be a place to have fun, and of course to create the opportunity for co-operators to give a little something back to the community.

I chose to get involved in Chain because I saw something that had mutually beneficial aspects. I get a warm feeling inside from the charity stuff we do and I get to meet new people. In return, others benefit from my actions. By joining Chain in its developing stages I also get to influence its growth and, in a short time, I have formed a bond with its progression, and now want it to realize its full potential.

Terry was asked to join the steering group on his return from Poland because of his enthusiasm and his experience in recruitment. The steering group now has seven members and we meet every two weeks.

What does the future hold for Chain?

We have secured increased funding for the next year and so want to continue to run one event per month. We will alternate events between evenings and lunch times in order to accommodate more people.

With Terry's help on the recruitment side, we hope to build on our existing membership base and improve on our attendance figures. We would like to have representatives in each building and preferably on each floor, people who can spread the word about events and encourage people to join in. We think seeing a friendly face will work better than an email over the computer system.

As last year was our first year, we found organisation was a challenge. This year we have set up an annual plan with specific times to review what we have done and keep ourselves on track. This forward planning ensures that there will be sufficient time to plan events, which will hopefully run smoothly.

Our first event for 2005 was to raise funds for the Tsunami disaster appeal. We ran a stand in the reception area of the Co-operative Group head office where we put together a Condolence Chain. People made a donation and wrote their message on the paper strip to those families who have lost friends and relatives. Each strip was strung together to make a chain. We managed to raise £328, which Chain will match from its own funds. Oxfam will be taking the money and the Condolence Chain out to the disaster area as it's involved in the mid to long-term rebuilding process.

Sweta Patel, India
Sweta is a student at Government College of Indian System of Medicine, Akhandanand Ayurvedic College, Ahmedabad, India.

11

NEHRU YUVA KENDRA SANGTHAN

An Umbrella for Youth Cooperatives in India

Sweta Patel

Nehru Yuva Kendra Sangathan (NYKS) is an autonomous organisation of the Department of Youth Affairs and Sports, Central Government, India. It has undertaken the promotion of the National Yuva Co-operative Society as a way to harness and to channel the productivity capacity of young people. Yuva means YOUTH.

The National Yuva Cooperative (NYC) was developed to encourage economic ventures by young people reflecting the spirit of self-help, participation and co-operation. It is based on the vision of a modern, powerful and technological India. The concept is to promote employment oriented and income generating activities through self help groups and micro-enterprises, with a view to helping young people to be economically productive and able to improve their quality of life; in the process they will help create a more self reliant and developed India.

Co-operatives are considered to be one of the most effective institutional mechanisms for developing a sustained economic development programme that empowers youth. In fact, India is considered an ocean of co-operatives where there are more than half a million cooperative societies with a total membership as high as 250 million members!

Youth of the country are highly idealistic and potent change agents and they constitute one third of the country's total population. A significant number of them, however, are caught in a vicious circle of poverty, illiteracy and unemployment. A large number of them do not have the opportunity to secure steady income generating positions. As a result, many of our youth are not in the mainstream of national development.

> **Co-operatives are considered to be one of the most effective institutional mechanisms for developing a sustained economic development programme that empowers youth.**

One of the major problems facing young people is that of increasing unemployment. While the Government is making efforts to create rural employment through various programmes, much emphasis will have to be placed on co-operative enterprises. This is why Nehru Yuva Kendra Sangathan is so important. It is one of the largest grass root level organisations in the world, having a network of nearly 2 million village-level youth clubs in the country.

NYKS is doing its best to provide employment to rural youth by providing vocational training in different trades, but more will have to be done to overcome the problems of unemployment among rural youth. Besides skill development, it will be necessary to provide counselling and finance as well as institutional and infrastructure support to youth to help them gain self-employment. It will require structural development intervention to enable them to assume responsibility for organising and managing co-operative micro-enterprise for their economic development. NYKS has undertaken to provide all possible support to launch youth co-operatives in the country.

The by-laws for the National Yuva Co-operative were registered with Central Registrar and Co-operative Societies, New Delhi, on 9th December 1999. Workshops were organized during the years 1999 and 2000 with the help of National Co-operative Development Corporation.

Membership:

The Membership of the NYC is open to:

- Individual young people,
- Youth clubs affiliated by Nehru Yuva Kendra Sangathan,
- National and State Level Co-operative Federations,
- Nehru Yuva Kendra Sangathan, and
- the Government of India and State Governments.

Associate memberships are available for individuals, societies and institutions having business transaction with NYC. They do not have, however, the right to vote, to participate in the management, or to share in its profits, assets and liabilities.

Activities:

- To promote and undertake employment oriented and income generating activities;
- To finance viable projects proposed by members;
- To provide services, raw materials, and assistance to young people;
- To create and provide marketing networks and support;
- To provide skill development training;
- To promote and support community service activities;
- To promote self-help groups, entrepreneurship and micro enterprises among youth;
- To promote e-commerce; and
- To promote production – agricultural, agro-based and rural-based industries.

NYKS has offices in about 500 districts of the country and NYC works within the NYKS network. This network has become the largest grass-root level organisation in the Asia-Pacific Region, catering to the needs of more than 6.4 million rural female and male youth enrolled in 179,000 village-based Youth Clubs. It provides education, training, health awareness, self-employment, financial assistance, etc. It generates activities for the over-all development of the rural communities through various activities and programmes. Each district NYKS has a trained cadre of District Youth Coordinators, National Service Volunteers and Youth Leaders. Its strength lies in the vast network of Youth Clubs that it serves at the grassroots level.

Regular programmes provided by NYKS include: Youth Club development programmes; vocational training programmes; awareness campaigns; work camps; celebration of National Youth Day and Youth Week; sports promotion programmes and cultural programmes.

Regular programmes provided by NYKS include: Youth Club development programmes; vocational training programmes; awareness campaigns; work camps; celebration of National Youth Day and Youth Week; sports promotion programmes and cultural programmes. In collaboration with UNICEF, NYKS has taken up a programme in Uttar Pradesh called "*youth action goal-2000*", which has five major components, known as *Panch Parameshwar*: namely, child education, health and immunization, drinking water, nutrition and family welfare. The programme is being implemented in 9,000 village *panchayats* in Uttar Pradesh. In collaboration with the Department of Women and Child Development, Government of India, NYKS is also implementing a project entitled *Mahila Samriddhi Yojana* in 40 districts of the country. Finally, NYKS in collaboration with National AIDS Control Organisation has taken up AIDS campaigns in forty-five districts of the north-eastern States.

NYKS also implements the following schemes of the Department of Youth Affairs and Sports: (a) youth development centres; (b) financial assistance to Youth Clubs; and (c) the National Service Volunteer Scheme.

Thus it can be seen, NYC and NYKS have undertaken a series of programmes related to youth development, ranging from sports, education, social services in normal and natural disaster time to self development and employment generation, institutional development. They are the implementing agency for many other national and international youth programmes and the umbrella for the widespread development of youth co-operatives.

12

Canadian

Co-operative Association (CCA):

Youth Working With Youth in
THE DEVELOPMENT OF
CO-OPERATIVES

Canada

It is hard to imagine compressing six months or a year of living and learning in a brand new environment into a scant 300 words. Yet that is exactly what six young people have done in the items that follow. With remarkable freshness and clarity, they capture some truths about co-operatives and about living outside of one's comfort zone. In many respects, those are the same qualities that young people bring to co-operatives.

Youth see co-operatives with fresh eyes, uncompromised by years of internal institutional politics or economic struggles. They see co-operative values for what they can and should be. They challenge older co-operators to also step out of their comfort zones to embrace the inevitable evolution of the co-operative movement. As one young writer so eloquently states "Culture is not static: it flows and adapts.... Co-operatives are a form of culture." These young people add yet another element that few older co-operators in Canada have experienced – a view of co-operatives in the context of the developing world.

Over the past eight years I have had the pleasure of helping ninety-five young Canadians step outside of their comfort zones in order to take on demanding internships with co-operatives in Asia, Africa and the Americas. I have watched with admiration as members of each successive group launch themselves into the unknown with courage and a remarkable desire to work and to learn. And each year, just as they have on these pages, they have provided me with fresh insight and inspiration.

John Julian
Director, International
Communications and Policy
Canadian Co-operative
Association

Kristi Zychowka, CCA Intern at Perpetual Help Credit Co-operative, Philippines

For six months I had the opportunity to work as a Youth Coordinator in a credit co-op in Dumaguete – a small, laid back city in the central region of the Philippines. It didn't take long for me to realize that for the staff, volunteers and members of the co-op, it wasn't simply a place to conduct one's banking – it was a community. Dumaguetenos spent countless hours planning for the co-op's future, recruiting and informing new members, serving the community with programmes such as medical outreach, and of course celebrating and socializing. The co-op was at the centre of the members' economic and social lives.

> It didn't take long for me to realize that for the staff, volunteers and members of the co-op, it wasn't simply a place to conduct one's banking – it was a community.

The activities of the co-op served a special purpose for its youth membership. On weekends, youth aged 15- 24 operated a small canteen business where they sold snacks to the participants of the co-op's pre-membership seminars. They organized youth workshops on co-operatives and saving, and at Christmas went carolling to raise funds for children at the local orphanage.

In a culture where self-reliance, independence and assertiveness aren't valued as they are in North America, these activities helped young people to develop confidence in addition to such skills as money management, event organisation, leadership, and public speaking. As well, according to the youth themselves, their activities served as a healthy distraction from the lure of drugs, alcohol and other negative influences. In my eyes, their hard work, dedication and hospitality served as an excellent example of the possibilities available when youth organize themselves within a co-operative framework.

Carmen Logie, CCA Intern at Ghana Co-operative Credit Union Association, 2003-2004

After my year developing youth co-operative programmes in Ghana, I find myself sifting through my memories like seashells on the beach, and tales shimmer as I hold them up to the sunlight for closer examination. These are the true stories we used to illuminate the benefits of saving money with the youth savings club programme run by the Ghana Co-operative Credit Unions Association.

One glimmering shell that immediately catches my eye is the story of the girl who saved a little pocket money each day throughout secondary school; upon graduation, she used her savings to buy her parents a deep freezer. With the money they made from selling iced water, her parents were able to send her to university.

> I see so many others sparkling in the light; the countless students who were able to pay their school fees through saving a little pocket money each day and thereby were not forced to drop out of school.

I choose another shiny stone: the case of a girl whose parents travelled, and, when they didn't come back on time, she withdrew her savings from the school to take care of her brothers and sisters.

I see so many others sparkling in the light; the countless students who were able to pay their school fees through saving a little pocket money each day and thereby were not forced to drop out of school.

Yes, these are inspirational and exceptional stories.

But something nags at me. These stories are all true, all incredible in their own ways, yet somehow the sensational overshadows the everyday co-operation underlying my experiences in Ghana. There is something deeper, and as I sift through the sand I realize that the sand is what contains, holds and shapes all of these beautiful things. The sand is what I must write about. So I close my eyes and wade through more memories.

It is a dark night, the cricket melodies fill the air, and there is some light coming from the moon. The young girl attaches the rope to her tin bucket, and gently lowers it into the well. Soon after, she draws it up, unties the rope, places the bucket on her head and walks carefully as she tries to keep her balance in the dark. The next girl in line takes her bucket, ties the rope, and lowers it into the well. And when I stop and look, I see a deep sense of co-operation, patience and acceptance being lifted with the water. At the same time the girls were collecting water for bathing, cooking and toileting, the young men gathered around a generator, taking turns winding it up in an effort to bring the lights back on. Working together to overcome the power failure at our youth savings club conference illuminated co-operation on a deeper level than I had ever experienced. And from the right angle, the water in the buckets shone and sparkled in the moonlight.

Alexis Keilen, CCA Intern in Mongolia, 2003

The power of co-operatives is easily apparent when they are the only entity in a small Mongolian village. I witnessed this with my own eyes when I embarked upon an International Youth Internship with the Canadian Co-operative Association. In the spring of 2003, I became a rural development assistant with the Canadian Co-operative

Association in the city of Ulaan Baatar, Mongolia. I was 26 years old, and this was my first experience doing international development work overseas.

It was an amazing opportunity, and it opened my eyes to the challenges that people face all over the world. People living in rural villages of Mongolia have to deal with harsh weather conditions, no running water or plumbing, no roads, and few modern conveniences. Most people in rural Mongolia survive by herding animals, usually sheep, cattle or horses. They use these animals for meat, milk and wool, and trade these products for any additional goods they may need. Unemployment is a constant problem in these villages, where there are few businesses hiring people to work for them. Mongolian villages are small and remote, with an average population of about 1000.

> It was an amazing opportunity, and it opened my eyes to the challenges that people face all over the world.

I saw these conditions in the 20 villages that my supervisor, Ingrid Fischer, and I visited as we conducted research on how co-operatives benefit communities in rural Mongolia. The benefits and advantages of co-operative development were immediately apparent.

The co-operatives in the villages are a source of income and social security for many people living in these remote areas. Many of the co-operatives we visited pooled their animal products and resources together to gain a source of social security. For example, only one member of the co-op would travel to a nearby city to trade or sell animals, or their by-products. They would sell the products, buy necessary goods, and then re-distribute them among the members of the co-op. The co-ops also created a social safety network for their members. It was amazing to see what a difference can be made when people work together for the common good.

Sara Groot, CCA intern with the Uganda Co-operative Alliance, 2004-2005

Working as a CCA/CIDA intern on the Youth Economic Empowerment Through Co-operative Projects (YEECO) with the Uganda Co-operative Alliance has given me the opportunity to witness first hand how youth are working together, using the co-operative model to try to improve their lives. All across Uganda, groups of youth are coming together to identify and meet their common needs, which range from the need for employment and an income, to other basic needs such as permanent housing and education.

Fruit drying is just one example of the creative enterprises that the youth groups are developing to increase their incomes. The members of the Kangulumira Produce and Marketing Co-operative have decided to add value to their individual pineapple crops by building solar driers for the members to use to process their produce into dried fruit. The dried pineapple is sold to a European exporter at a much higher price than fresh pineapples.

The role of YEECO is to strengthen these youth groups and to help them build the capacity to succeed. The YEECO training programme has two main goals: to provide knowledge of technical skills (such as solar-dried fruit) and to build leadership and confidence, which will help youth to develop and use their skills to their fullest potential.

> It has been a challenge to adapt my skills to another culture and setting, but it has given me the opportunity to learn from others and explore different approaches to doing things.

I have been designing and leading workshops on peer education to encourage youth group members to recognizing the value of the experiences they possess, and to help them share these experiences so they can learn from each other.

This internship is allowing me to practice and improve upon participatory training techniques and workshop planning. It has been a challenge to adapt my skills to another culture and setting, but it has given me the opportunity to learn from others and explore different approaches to doing things.

Julia Smith, CCA intern with International Co-operative Alliance Regional Office for Africa, Kenya, 2004-2005

My feet are slowly sliding from beneath me as the mud slips down the hill. Clutching my notepad and trying not to miss a word my host, a co-op coffee farmer in Kenya, is saying, I steady myself on the edge of a terrace. The hills surrounding me are carved into steps, to conserve the little bit of rain that falls on the coffee plants here in the Machakos region, just southeast of Nairobi.

It is not the first time I've felt I was about to lose my footing, literally and figuratively speaking. Since I arrived in Kenya on a Canadian Co-operative Association internship, I've felt the ground shift beneath me many times. In four days of field research in Machakos I learned more than I did in four years of university.

I'm in Machakos to conduct a gender analysis of a community development project that was carried out with a co-operative here. As I discuss gender equity with the all male co-op board, or with a group of widows who ignore the issues I bring up and favour discussions on the practicalities of water and chickens, or with the individual coffee farmer in front of me, I find myself continually questioning my assumptions and understandings of gender within the co-operative context. Sometimes I notice the people I'm speaking with are experiencing the same uneasiness, that my presence and words influence their concepts concerning gender a little and attitudes are beginning to change.

These moments give me a thrill. As the coffee farmer and I each slip a little in our understanding we are, in a small and clumsy way, co-operating towards change.

Katie Didyk, CCA Intern with the Uganda Co-operative Alliance, 2004-2005

Rule number one: do not arrive and think you are going to single-handedly change the world. It has never happened this way and it never will. I have learned through my internship as the Gender Officer with the Uganda Co-operative Alliance, that strength in numbers, encouraging people with similar values, goals and beliefs, is how to really make changes for the better.

Co-operatives capitalize and build on the strengths of communities, especially the will and efforts of people to work together for a greater gain. I am seeing the relationships between women and men re-evaluated and changed through learning and applying their knowledge of gender balance and mainstreaming, and how this can form positive and sustainable practices for the future.

> I have learned through my internship as the Gender Officer with the Uganda Co-operative Alliance, that strength in numbers, encouraging people with similar values, goals and beliefs, is how to really make changes for the better.

The discourse of gender is a hot topic in the co-operative movement. Members are eager to learn, educate and combine modernized practices without entirely removing their own cultural value system. This is what I am taking advantage of through my internship; the level of involvement and support for equality at all levels within the co-operative movement.

Working within the gender field in Uganda has provided me with insights into Africa and into the stronghold of culture. It is difficult sometimes for me to separate myself from my culture and upbringing, in order to understand the culture here. There have been moments throughout my internship when I could see the gender disparities so clear but knew that a solution, one that may be ideal in Canada, would not be effective here. I think this has been the frustrating aspect of working in this field; resisting the urge to apply a "top down" approach, so widely known in the development past.

Culture is not static; it changes, flows and adapts with the growing need and behaviours of a community. Co-operatives are a form of culture. They represent the people as a whole, and are guided by beliefs and values, some inherent, some external. I feel like I have become a part of something much bigger, something that will continue to be strong, even after I have left, when my "work here is done". Co-operatives are the means to an end in Africa, the end being an alleviation of poverty for many. In my eyes, this is a bright future.

Oscar Velasquez Carreño, Columbia

Oscar is an active member of the National Youth Co-operative Network in Colombia.

13

National Youth
CO-OPERATIVE
NETWORK

Oscar Velasquez Carreño

Members: The organisation has 32 members.

Purpose: The National Youth Co-operative Network organises projects and activities to promote co-operativism among youth.

Service Area: The organisation serves Bogotá (Capital of Columbia, Cundinamarca Department), Cali (Valle Department), Medellín (Antioquia Department) and Bucaramanga (Santander Department).

Identified Needs

The organisation has identified the following needs:

- More youth participation in the operation of the co-operatives;
- Leadership succession planning within the co-operatives by encouraging intergenerational connections; and
- More information sessions about co-operative issues within the community in general and among the people who make up the co-operative sector in particular.

Context Within Which the Network Evolved

Meetings in which young Columbians participated (including those who currently constitute the NETWORK) were held in Bogotá (1998), México (1998), Korea (2001) Cajicá (2003), Buenos Aires (2004) and Cajicá (2004).

In 1998 the first National Youth Co-operative Workshop, which examined how young people can work in innovative ways, was held in Bogotá. Fundequidad supported the workshop.

In 1998 at the Regional Conference of the International Co-operative Alliance (ICA) of the Americas in México it was concluded that the concerns that most affected youth (apart from ecology) were issues of employment, education, and participation in co-operatives.

In October 2001, young delegates of more than 20 countries attended a one-day seminar under the framework of the World Conference of the ICA in Seoul, Korea. Speakers included Roberto Rodríguez, then president of the ICA, and Ian MacPherson of the University of Victoria.

In December 2003, Seguros la Equidad and Fundequidad, organised a meeting with young co-operative leaders in Cajicá, Cundinamarca, to organize what today is the NATIONAL YOUTH CO-OPERATIVE NETWORK.

In November 2004, the participants of the Latin America Meeting of Young Co-operativists of the ICA in Buenos Aires,

MEMBERS OF THE NATIONAL YOUTH CO-OPERATIVE NETWORK

ANTIOQUIA CHAPTER

SANTANDER CHAPTER

VALLE CHAPTER

BOGOTÁ CHAPTER

Argentina, concluded that young people should be included in a coherent and constant political process within co-operatives.

In December of 2004, the second meeting of the NATIONAL YOUTH CO-OPERATIVE NETWORK took place. It considered issues of legality, organization and communication and discussed possible future projects. The young people reaffirmed their commitment to contribute their abilities and knowledge to the development of the organisation.

The NETWORK will be a legally constituted youth organisation that brings together regional interests for national promotion and strengthening of the commitment to solidarity among young people.

Mission

The NETWORK is an autonomous youth organisation promoting the co-operative movement through the participation, education, and employment of Columbian youth.

Model

In order to develop national unity, the NATIONAL YOUTH CO-OPERATIVE NETWORK functions as an organisation based on the support of regional chapters and the trust of its members.

Needs

The needs of the young people in the NETWORK in Columbia are to have opportunities for education and employment for themselves within their communities. They aspire to participate actively in the democratic processes of the co-operatives and of society.

NETWORK MEMBERS WITH
DR. PALACINO, PRESIDENT ICA-AMERICAS

Knowledge of Needs

In Columbia the executive boards of some co-operatives have a serious and coherent commitment to involving youth in their operations. Nevertheless, the great majority of organisations in the sector have yet to promote an awareness of co-operativism and an understanding of the solidarity philosophy among young people.

That is why we recognised the need to form an autonomous organisation of young people that can work with other organisations in the co-operative sector to help promote co-operative identity from the grassroots level.

Benefits

- Involves young people in the co-operative movement
- Improves training and employment opportunities for NETWORK members
- Encourages political participation in Columbian society
- Provides communication channels to articulate youth perspectives in co-operatives
- Promotes co-operative philosophy
- Proposes and develops social projects with co-operatives

Obstacles

- Lack of information concerning legal, organisational, and administrative issues within co-operatives by the youngest members of the organisation
- Weak communication among members, although ways to do so are available (internet, cellular telephone system)

Facilitating Aspects of Development

- The workgroup has informal dynamics motivated and based on teamwork
- NETWORK members support the philosophy of co-operativism
- The support and backing of representative co-operatives within the movement in Columbia

Strategies of the Organisation

We intend to continue our work of building and consolidating the NETWORK in three ways:

1. Consolidate chapters
2. Consolidate the National Network
3. Promote benefits and services

NETWORK IN CAJICÁ- CUNDINAMARCA

Structure of the Organisation:

The organisation works in chapters. Four are presently being formed (Bogotá, Bucaramanga, Cali, and Medellín), and they are all are guided by the value system and the processes described above.

Kandarp Patel, India

Kandarp Patel is a student of Government Engineering College, Gandhinagar, India.

14

THE GUJARAT UNIVERSITY
Central Consumers'
Cooperative Stores Limited

Kandarp Patel

Youth represent the most vibrant section of any society and play a pivotal role in its socio-economic changes and development. A nation can progress only when the energy of youth is channelled into constructive work. It is imperative that youth be given a major role in the process of development.

In India, young people account for nearly one-third of the total population: i.e., 350 million out of a total population of 1.1 billion. In an effort to fulfill the aspirations of this group and to empower them as active and constructive agents of positive change, the National Service Scheme, popularly known as NSS, was launched in Gandhi's Birth Centenary Year, 1969. It is active within 37 universities and involves 40,000 students in programmes concerned with developing personality through community service. Its aims are:

- to encourage youth to respect the principles and values enshrined in the Constitution of India;
- to promote an awareness of the historical heritage of the nation;
- to help develop the qualities of discipline, self-reliance, justice and fair play; and
- to help students develop their personality as they pursue their education.

Chapter IV of the Indian Constitution provides insight and direction for the State to empower youth (as well as other weaker sections of society) through co-operatives. India is historically a welfare state that has always given a high priority to educating children and to helping them to grow in a well-rounded way. Students have been woven into the fabric of the Indian co-operative movement, as is evident in the following table on student co-operatives in India.

STUDENT'S CO-OPERATIVES IN INDIA

Number of Co-operatives: 3948	
Membership: 19,35,296	
Students – 89.7%	
Teachers – 4.01%	
Others – 6.27%	
(Amounts in Million INR)	
Working Capital:	471
Deposits:	53.58
Reserves:	29.54
Government Participation:	70.8%
Total Sale:	**514.1 million**

Source: NCUI Bulletin – A profile of Indian Cooperatives in the year 2001.

As part of state policy, and within the traditions and needs indicated above, the Gujarat University Central Consumers' Cooperative Stores Limited was established in the year 1969 at Ahmedabad, Gujarat State of India. Gujarat was the birthplace of Mahatma Gandhi, the Father of the Nation and the champion of its youth. He established one University in the city of Ahmedabad, namely Gujarat Vidhyapith, and he worked in

Ahmedabad during the famous freedom struggle. The Gujarat University Central Consumers' Co-operative Stores Limited (henceforth described as the Society) was incorporated under the guidance of the then vice chancellor of the university. The students were encouraged to register as members and to participate in the affairs of the Society.

The Society was primarily established to supply such necessities as stationery, grains, provisions, clothes and other daily needs. It was established in an era of severe shortages of food, oil, clothes and provisions; a time of rationing and shortages. It was a period when the area in which the university is located (the western part of the city of Ahmedabad) was comparatively remote, a place where the few shopkeepers who were there openly exploited the students. The university teachers and student leaders sympathized with the needs of the students and urged the university authorities to help the co-operative develop.

The then vice chancellor and other office bearers, influenced by Gandhian philosophy, immediately reacted to the problem and inspired students to form their own co-operative. The University provided infrastructure as well as administrative, political and financial support in starting the co-operative and the teachers and other staff members were allowed to be members. The co-operative started with only 300 members, 20 of them institutional members, such as university press staff and teachers.

> [The Society] was established in an era of severe shortages of food, oil, clothes and provisions; a time of rationing and shortages. It was a period when the area in which the university is located (the western part of the city of Ahmedabad) was comparatively remote, a place where the few shopkeepers who were there openly exploited the students.

At the end of financial year 2004, there were 4600 members, including 250 institutional members. The co-operative particularly encouraged female students to join as members, but they do not play a dominant role in its affairs.

The Society is led by a board of 11 directors, six elected by the students and five by staff and institutional members. The present chairman of the board is Mr. Narhari Amin, a former Deputy Chairman of the State of Gujarat and a senate member of the university. He is an educationist and well-known philanthropist. Under the board, various committees address special issues and work for the over-all development and growth of the society and its members.

The Society is responsible for the operation of more than 160 hostel and staff quarters for employees of the University. It is engaged in supplying books, stationery, woollen cloths, food grains, pulses, oils, provisions and other supplies to the students and employees of University. It purchases as much as possible from fair trade shops and co-operative wholesales. A committee under the guidance of a senate member finalizes the purchases and the University gives priority to the society for any purchases or sales.

Financial performance:

highlights of the Society for 2002-2003 and 2003-2004

(Amount in INR)

Sr. No.	Particular	2002-2003	2003-2004
1	Sale – Provision	166231	166156
2	Sale – Grains	580883	1045871
3	Sale – Stationery	2149802	407454
4	Sale – Clothes	183669	302688
5	Sale – Books	2443356	1540010
6	Sale University forms	5146626	4207109
7	Sale University stationery		2370500
8	SALE	10670567	10039789
9	Gross Profit	373198	349544
10	Net profit	114396	82440
11	Equity capital	52440	52640
12	Reserve	183769	212468
13	Bank Loan	99864	---

* source – Annual Report of the Society

The co-operative model can help build the confidence of young people, and it can enhance students' capacity building as they shape their careers and futures. It is the responsibility of large well-established institutes, such as the university, to support the creation and growth of co-operatives as a way of helping youth to develop. By doing so, they also ensure that students are treated fairly in a growing global economy and they can insist that co-operatives engage in fair and ethical trade. The present management of the university and the co-operative are helping students to adapt to the context and environment of our times. They are doing so by encouraging students to play a role in the co-operative and to learn by doing so, as well as through the youth awareness programmes that the Society operates. They have confidence in the co-operative model, want to share it with young people, and are helping to ensure that globalisation means global co-operation.

Allan Bartolcic, Canada

Allan Bartolcic is the Director of Youth & Community Development for the Rural Education and Development Association in Edmonton, Alberta, Canada.

15

REDA

Co-operative
Youth Program

Allan Bartolcic

The REDA Co-operative Youth Program is A Unique Alberta Youth Experience. The REDA Co-operative Youth Program is one of several programmes s offered by the Rural Education and Development Association (REDA). REDA is a private, non-profit continuing education organisation dedicated to providing human resource training and programme development

The first Co-operative Youth Program was held at Elk Island National Park at Camp Agape in 1961, attracting 91 young people between the ages of sixteen and twenty from rural Alberta. It was intended to develop leadership skills and co-operative attitudes in youth, and to encourage their active involvement in the community. The

PROGRAM PARTICIPANTS LEARNING THE VALUE OF CO-OPERATION

first programme held at Goldeye Centre was in the summer of 1962. The programme covered topics such as Co-operative organizations, farm family business agreements, water safety and agriculture.

The REDA Co-operative Youth Program has seen several changes over the past few decades, including a move away from a rural youth focus, an increase in urban participants, and additional leadership curriculum content. Amidst all the changes, the principles the programme was founded on still remain. The REDA Co-operative Youth Program continues to create awareness and understanding in youth about co-operative ideals, leadership development, and the importance of community and the agriculture industry.

Some specific learning outcomes from the programme include:

- Working with people with different personalities
- Problem-solving techniques in groups
- Conflict management in groups
- Assertive communication skills
- Improved self confidence

This experiential seven day programme continues to take place at Goldeye Centre and runs over seven weeks of the summer, typically from late June to early August. There are three phases, and each caters to a different age group and offers a varied program.

Approximately 350 participants go through the programme each summer, with a maximum of fifty to fifty-five participants accommodated at one time.

The REDA Co-operative Youth Program exists to serve the belief held by REDA's stakeholders that the future of their organisations and communities are the youth of today. Consequently, youth will need to develop the skills to be effective in their organisations and communities.

Our Mission

We are committed to providing an innovative learning environment that fosters the development of leadership skills and co-operative ideals in youth to benefit our communities.

Our Vision

The Co-operative Youth Program will be a dynamic leadership programme of choice, responsive to the needs of Alberta youth, member organizations and communities, and recognized for its contributions to society.

REDA CO-OPERATIVE YOUTH PROGRAM PARTICIPANTS

Values and Beliefs

The REDA Co-operative Youth Program has a statement of Values and Beliefs to guide the programmes operations. It represents the essence of the programme and, allows both staff and participants to gauge their actions and decisions.

The REDA Co-operative Youth Programs Values and Beliefs Statements are:

Co-operation: By pooling our resources we create results greater than the sum of the individual parts. Co-operation enables us to succeed through mutual self help and the strength of the co-operating members.

Respect: We not only accept differences amongst individuals and groups, but we celebrate the richness this diversity brings to our lives.

Integrity: We are forthright in our motives. Through honest, open communications we build and maintain trust.

Personal Growth: Our actions contribute to the individual's development. By enhancing the individual's abilities and confidence he or she is empowered to reach his or her potential.

Learning: Learning starts where the individual is at and should result in positive changes in her or his life and the lives of those around her or him. Challenging experiences combined with success stimulate learning.

FANTASTIC FRIENDSHIPS ARE FORMED AT CAMP

Community: Wherever we connect to others we have responsibilities to care for each other and give back to our communities without expectation of direct benefits.

Safety: The physical and emotional well-being of youth is placed in our hands. We diligently uphold that trust and responsibility.

Professionalism: We only undertake approved activities in which we are capable. We are ethical and reliable. The interests of youth come before our own.

PIRATES NEED TO LEARN ABOUT CO-OPERATION TOO

History of the Youth Programme

"This is a pioneer camp, but it has been so successful that the campers hope the idea will spread to other districts in Alberta", stated Donna Cropley, President of the Students Council at the Youth Camp sponsored by the Farmers Union of Alberta and Co-operative Development Association (FUA & CDA), June 30 - July 6, 1961. Held at Camp Agape in Elk Island National Park...the pilot project attracted 41 young people ages sixteen to twenty.

In 1958, Goldeye Lake had been chosen as the site of a training camp designed to develop qualities of leadership and citizenship in the young people of rural Alberta.

The first annual Farmers Union of Alberta (F.U.A.) & C.D.A. Rural Young Peoples Camp was held at Goldeye Camp, July 29 - August 3, 1962. The programme covered such topics as: co-operative organisations, family farm business agreements, water safety, junior F.U.A. and agriculture in other lands. The fee, which covered room and board and transportation from central points, was $20 for the week.

> The Co-operative Youth Program still endeavours to create awareness and understanding in youth about co-operatives, leadership, citizenship and the importance of the farm organisation. Sponsors of the programme recognize the ever-continuing need to develop our future community leaders.

By 1964, four one-week Teen Camps were being held at Goldeye and one Teen Camp at Fairview College. Total attendance was 291. Content covered co-operatives, farm organisations, leadership skills, citizenship and recreation. A one-week Grad Seminar was held for thirty-four participants and included more in-depth subject areas from teen Camps plus human relations, communications and business aspects of farming.

In 1967 three Youth Seminars replaced the five Teen Camps. Shortly afterwards, REDA was formed and it took on the responsibilities of the previous F.U. & C.D.A. Activities assumed by REDA included the Co-operative Youth Program.

By 1974, the REDA Co-operative Youth Program had taken the form of three levels. Two teen camps were offered for ages fourteen and fifteen. Teens enjoyed recreational and outdoor education. They learned to do things in co-operative styles and they learned about living together as a community. Two Youth Seminars for ages sixteen to eighteen allowed young people to explore co-operatives, rural change and development and decision making and personal goal setting. The Grad Seminar was directed toward young adults soon to be on their own. Participants learned about finding a place to live and adjusting to new surroundings. Environmental Concerns were also addressed. 293 participants paid or found sponsorship for the $45 cost of attending.

The past two decades has brought about some further changes. Content of the programme adjusts according to needs and the fee is now over $350. Yet, amidst all the changes in the numbers and programs, some basics still hold true. The Co-operative Youth Program still endeavours to create awareness and understanding in youth about co-operatives, leadership, citizenship and the importance of the farm organisation. Sponsors of the programme recognize the ever-continuing need to develop our future community leaders.

When asked what people remember most about their participation at the Co-operative Youth Program, the vast majority will reply friends. Since the very first years the most outstanding quality has been making new and very dear friends.

16

Youth and International Development:

Motivating the Next Generation

Information provided by the World Council of Credit Unions, Inc.

First introduced in 2001, World Council of Credit Union's Young Credit Union Professionals Program (WYCUP) encourages credit union organizations to commit to involving youth and young professionals in national and international credit union movements.

Upon the board's approval of the program, chief operating officer Brian Branch commented, "I'm very excited by the commitment of the board of directors to set the example for credit union movements to involve the next generation in our international activities. "This is a great way to motivate the next generation to get involved in and commit to the credit union movement."

> *"* WYCUP encourages credit union organizations to commit to involving youth and young professionals in national and international credit union movements. *"*

By recognizing and promoting the next generation of leaders in the international system WOCCU aims to ensure the future sustainability of the international credit union system. Credit unions and credit union organizations affiliated with World Council are encouraged to participate in this aim by identifying and nominating their next generation of credit union leaders, aged 35 and under, to compete for the WYCUP scholarship, an all expense-paid opportunity to attend the World Credit Union Conference the following year. Several credit union organizations have organized national competitions to select their representative most deserving of sponsorship to compete in this international forum and others are fortunate enough to have the funds to send multiple nominees.

WOCCU's World Credit Union Conference offers the ideal environment for young professionals to broaden their perspectives on the international credit union movement, learn about the newest trends in credit union development and network with other credit union leaders, particularly their young professional peers. WYCUP nominees are uniquely recognized at the conference and are invited to take part in events organized specifically for those ages 35 and under. Prior conference locations include: France, Poland, Australia, and the Bahamas. Winners of the 2004 Scholarship will attend this year's conference in Rome, Italy, and in 2006 nominees will head to Dublin, Ireland.

The WYCUP committee looks to reward those individuals who have already made a significant contribution to the development of their credit union, regional or national credit union system and also have the potential contribute to the international credit union movement. "We will be looking specifically at the nominees' personal commitment to fostering and engaging youth involvement in the credit union movements of their respective countries," 2004 WYCYP chairman Gregorz Bierecki said of the committee's role.

In its first year, WYCUP nominees numbered twenty-three individuals from nine different countries. In following three years, the number of nominees increased to over thirty individuals from as many as twelve different countries. "The number of nominations received from credit union organizations throughout the world proves that there is a great need for such an initiative to be championed by WOCCU," said Bierecki. "We aim to effectively assist young professionals in recognizing genuine career opportunities and gradually assuming leadership positions within the international credit union movement."

> WOCCU's World Credit Union Conference offers the ideal environment for young professionals to broaden their perspectives on the international credit union movement, learn about the newest trends in credit union development and network with other credit union leaders, particularly their young professional peers.

Winners have hailed from locations as diverse as Australia, the Bahamas, Canada, Ireland, Jamaica, Malawi, New Zealand, Peru, Poland, Scotland, Trinidad, and the United States. "Being a WYCUP participant was one of the most rewarding career experiences for me," declared 2003 WYCUP scholarship winner Malcolm Stoffman, marketing and communications manager of Teachers Credit Union in Hamilton, Ontario, Canada. "It was a one of a kind opportunity to sit down with managers, CEOs and board chairmen of national and international organizations to discuss the challenges facing young leaders today. Participating in the WYCUP program also provided me with a number of additional opportunities. Since winning the WYCUP scholarship, I have been asked to speak on youth issues at credit union events and invited to join a cooperative management program in England."

Skott Pope, vice president of education and development for Washington Credit Union League and 2002 WYCUP scholarship winner, said, "Participating in the WYCUP program was the highlight of my career. The connections I have made with credit union professionals around the world help keep me motivated, have given me new ideas to help my organization and have made me feel like I'm connected to the greater good of the movement. I cannot express the difference that it has made in both my personal and professional life."

> The WYCUP committee looks to reward those individuals who have already made a significant contribution to the development of their credit union, regional or national credit union system and also have the potential contribute to the international credit union movement.

PART FOUR:

Conclusions and Recommendations

Conclusions

1. The papers and case studies included in this book are largely the result of contacts made through an emerging youth network that has been developing over the last five years, one that will continue to grow, judged by the successes of the ICA's youth group and the development of international youth conferences associated with ICA and national co-operative gatherings. The success of the Building Co-operative Futures conferences, started at the University of Victoria in 2003, continued in Alberta and Saskatchewan in the two following years and planned for Manchester in 2006, also suggests the interest young people have in furthering their understanding of co-operative strategies for addressing contemporary issues.

2. Many young people, when the option is explained and available to them, are attracted to the co-operative model, its values and principles. They prize its emphasis on job fulfilment, democratic structures and commitment to community responsibility. They see co-operatives as places that prize autonomy, collaborative behaviour, team-building, responsible behaviour and greater accountability. They are also consistent in their appreciation: they admire most the co-operatives that walk the walk as well as talk the talk. They have an instinctive desire to operate their own organisations; they do not appreciate being patronized. Once they have the opportunity, as the papers and case studies abundantly testify, the personal experiences can be among the richest of their lives, creating careers, forming lifetime friendships, and opening doors to other cultures.

3. The papers and case studies are indicative of the situation regarding youth involvement in co-operatives, but they are not a systematic or complete analysis of an important but weakly comprehended dimension of the contemporary co-operative experience. The editors are convinced that there are many, many more examples of youth involvement in co-operatives happening around the world, but that the networks that might inform and sustain them are weak and need support. Hopefully, in another book or through one or more websites, their stories will become known for the benefit of others interested in pursuing the co-operative option or of people within co-operative movements interested in expanding youth participation in co-operative enterprise.

4. Broadly speaking, this volume reveals two kinds of youth involvement in co-operatives. The first is the kind of co-operative that is essentially the result of independent efforts by young people. As the case studies reveal, however, this is a rather arbitrary distinction; as in the past with most kinds of co-operatives (including most of those now well-established and flourishing), new co-operatives have been helped by other co-ops, government support, or assistance from like-minded movements. Nevertheless, there are some co-operatives among young people that have achieved a high degree of independence and that have essentially started out of the efforts of young people independent of others. Such co-ops seem qualitatively to be different from those that were started under the umbrella of established co-operative institutions or networks.

The second kind of involvement is that which results from efforts by established co-operatives to encourage youth participation. Several of the case studies reveal that many co-operative organisations have undertaken, and are undertaking, significant and useful work in trying to encourage youth participation in their organisations or in developing new co-operatives. They are to be commended for these efforts, which vary in purpose and structure considerably. The case studies reveal that any of several approaches can be successful and one should not hasten to judge them or necessarily prefer one over another. The point is that such efforts emerge out of different geopolitical and institutional frameworks and they are the results of the dominant ideological and cultural perspectives that dominate in given societies or among specific memberships and leadership cadres. That does not mean, however, that co-operatives cannot learn from what others are doing; in fact, we hope that one of the outcomes of this book will be a more thorough and complete discussion among co-operatives about how they can best activate and serve the youth in their midst.

5. Several of the case studies demonstrate that involvement in co-operatives provides an opportunity for young people to learn how to become entrepreneurs. This is most evident in the cases from the southern parts of the globe, where the co-operative model permits the accumulation of financial, social and human resources that would otherwise be impossible.

6. There is a need for further and more in-depth research to understand if these differences are indeed substantial and, if they are, what that means for successful youth applications of the co-operative model. In fact, these case studies offer numerous opportunities for further research, opportunities that we hope will particularly attract young researchers and activists.

7. There is a need for further research to understand more completely what kinds of issues young people encounter as they try to develop formal co-operatives. Are they different issues from those that confront more senior, more experienced, people undertaking similar objectives? Is there a need for a different or more intensive training programme? Can the education system be expected to meet those needs? If so, what does the educational system require in the way of teaching and training materials to undertake that task? What more can we learn from the experiences of such programmes as the institutions at the University of Massachusetts, whose work is briefly described in this book.

8. The paper and case studies indicate that most young people have to be in the right place at the right time to learn about co-operatives. Despite efforts made by some co-operatives to reach out to young people, it is clear that the message is not being widely received. Clearly, too, and most importantly, except for rare circumstances (such as in Malaysia), they do not learn about the co-operative model through their educational institutions. Several case studies also reveal that the few existing educational systems that do address co-operative themes merely adapt programmes designed for private enterprise without grounding in co-operative philosophy and experience.

This educational void is a question that governments and co-operative organisations need to address in the interests of providing a full and fair level playing field for the development of different kinds of economic and social institutions. There is a need for the development of teaching resources and programmes for engaging young people in the appropriate study of co-operatives within educational institutions, an initiative that needs to be initiated or reinvigorated within local, national and co-operative movements and addressed within the international organisations associated with the movement.

9. One clear issue that reappears in the case studies is the need for funding, a common issue in the formation of new co-operatives, but perhaps exacerbated with the complexities of lending to young people. Perhaps this is an opportunity for the more widespread application of some creative lending approaches, such as that being developed in South Africa or in India. Maybe there is a way to adapt more fully the techniques of peer lending and micro credit, adapted specifically to youth needs. Maybe more financial institutions can develop special lending programmes for young people, such as that used by Vancity Credit Union.

10. There are similarities within the youth initiatives described in these papers. Perhaps the most common one is that young people are interested in co-operatives primarily for the purpose of securing employment and building careers. That is arguably the main difference between co-operatives started essentially by young people and some of the co-operative programmes undertaken by well-established co-operatives. Another obvious similarity is the high level of pride and enthusiasm the young people involved with co-operatives have shown in their activities. In several instances, the enthusiasm can only be described as "catching" and inspirational. A third commonality is a deep interest in the environment: it is a clear motivation behind several of the case studies and it constantly reappears at youth gatherings. The fourth is a deep concern for community issues…a perspective that challenges established co-operatives, as it should. The most agonizing and difficult of these community challenges, of course, is the HIV/AIDS pandemic in Africa, but also evident in cases from other parts of the world as well.

11. There are also profound differences and it would be a mistake to think that there is a "one size fits all" approach to how young people might be encouraged to think about and, as they deem appropriate, use the co-operative model. The most obvious difference lies in culture. That is partly why international exchanges and internships are so valuable: young people learn from each other, understand that there is not just one way to accomplish a task, appreciate that there are different cultural, religious and social ways to understand and to accomplish…not just a banal abstraction but a genuine appreciation of difference. That is why the initiatives must emerge out of local circumstances and meet needs that youth define for themselves.

12. Young people want to have a choice in pursuing their objectives. They want to have the co-operative option as one of those choices, but the impediments to them having that choice, the lack of opportunities within educational institutions, the complexities in starting co-operatives, the challenges in becoming involved in existing co-operatives, all limit their possibilities.

13. The papers and case studies reveal an abundance of experience among young people who have tried to use the co-operative model. Several lessons have been learned, which might be summarized as follows, youth to youth.

- Become involved in existing co-operatives in whatever ways are open to you.
- Have the confidence to start your own co-operative…young people do it all the time and for all kinds of reasons.
- Develop a mutually supportive group of people to start the co-operative.
- Do not try to grow too fast.
- Establish strong ties with your community…however you define it.
- Involve all members of the co-operative in the decision-making processes.
- Welcome support, but not interference, from other organisations.
- Understand the distinct roles for members, elected leaders and employees.
- Develop a well-researched feasibility study.
- Develop a well-researched business plan and look for help in preparing it.
- Good funding ensures strong commitments.
- Understand, respect and apply the co-operative principles and adhere to co-operative values.
- Think carefully about who is elected to provide leadership.
- Co-operatives established within schools need the strong support of the administration and teachers.
- The business must be managed prudently.
- Develop a training programme to meet the needs of members, elected leaders, managers and employees.
- Like other co-operatives, youth co-operatives must consider their relationships with their communities.
- It is very important that governments and other co-operatives understand and view positively the possibilities of co-operative action.
- Every effort should be made to enlist the support of other co-operatives in the community.
- Make time for fun. Be tolerant. Be flexible.

14. As with their predecessors in earlier generations, today's youth are starting co-operatives that can provide the beginnings of lifetime careers within the co-operative sector or that will provide valuable opportunities to enter the job market and to develop their entrepreneurial skills. They too can "grow older", perhaps even old, within the organisations they have helped build or are building; they can move on, carrying with them valuable lessons for whatever field of activity they enter.

Recommendations

The work started in this project, understanding the possibilities and issues confronting young people wishing to engage the co-operative movement, should be expanded and developed more systematically. To further this objective, we make the following recommendations.

1. International organisations, such as the International Co-operative Alliance and the International Labour Organisation, should continue and expand as possible their recently developed initiatives to encourage greater youth involvement in existing co-operatives and in the development of their own co-operatives. National, regional and local organisations engaged in youth programmes should be encouraged to continue that work and be recognized for it. In fact, it is noticeable that youth programmes are not widely acknowledged and celebrated within the co-operative movement by awards and recognition ceremonies (the main exception being parts of Asia).

2. This book should be the beginning of a general effort to find out more about youth programmes within established co-operatives and about co-operatives that young people have established, or are establishing, by themselves for their own purposes. This is a challenge to the general academic community, within and without universities, and, especially to young people. Co-operative researchers, particularly the International Co-operative Research Committee of the International Co-operative Alliance and its regional affiliates, should encourage participation by young people involved in developing co-operatives at their meetings. There are research issues of obvious importance in this area, such as understanding better the specific needs of youth, appraising the effectiveness of existing programmes, addressing funding issues, and understanding better how educational systems can meet the needs of youth developing co-operatives.

3. The information gathered through future research, as well as research previously undertaken but generally unknown, should be made available on various websites, national, regional, sectoral, and international with the co-operative movement. It should also be made available through the Co-operative Learning Centre being developed by the International Co-operative Alliance, the International Labour Office and the British Columbia Institute for Co-operative Studies. A special web page is being developed for this purpose.

4. Co-operative organizations, at the local, national, regional and international levels, regularly review their youth activities to see if there are ways that they can be improved and further developed. They should encourage and sponsor youth workshops, seminars and publications. They should help in the development of strong youth networks.

5. Local, national, regional and international co-operative organisations, teachers and researchers need to address systematically how the study of co-operatives and co-operative thought can be more effectively and accurately presented in elementary, secondary, post-secondary, technical and adult education programmes.